**Mahamba Wa-ibera Evariste**

# God's plans and purposes for your life

Mahamba Wa-ibera Evariste

# God's plans and purposes for your life

Blessed Hope Publishing

**Imprint**



Cover image: www.ingimage.com

Publisher:
Blessed Hope Publishing
is a trademark of
Dodo Books Indian Ocean Ltd. and OmniScriptum S.R.L publishing group

120 High Road, East Finchley, London, N2 9ED, United Kingdom
Str. Armeneasca 28/1, office 1, Chisinau MD-2012, Republic of Moldova, Europe
Printed at: see last page
**ISBN: 978-620-4-18817-1**

# GOD'S PLANS AND PURPOSES FOR YOUR LIFE

**By Mahamba Wa-ibera Evariste**

**Founder and Leading Pastor**
**Ebenezer Evangelical Church International**
**BENI, DEMOCRATIC REPUBLIC OF CONGO**

**Acknowledgements**

This book is dedicated to all those ministers of the Word who are committed in mentoring future servants of God - especially Rev James Robinette (Mission Africa: the ministry of Jim +Kappy, USA) whom God is using to encourage me in ministry and the writing of books. He has assured me that writing is a much needed gift for the Church and I believe that God has given me the gift of writing books. I am very glad to write my first book which is a result of his many encouraging words.

Special thanks to my Almighty God who has given this gift of writing books and articles.

Special thanks to Rodney W. Francis (Founder and Director of the Gospel Faith Messenger Ministry, New Zealand) for mentoring me, and also for his guidance while I have been writing this book and other articles.

My eternal thanks go also to my wife Kasoki Nguru Elizabeth who is a great support for me and the ministry that I am coordinating.

I am grateful for all those who have supported this work in their daily prayers - especially Rev Russell Daniels ( in Uganda of the Independent Baptist of USA, Grace Baptist Church in Saint Charles, Missouri , of the Baptist Bible Fellowship in USA ), Tina Lee (New Heart Mission Church, USA), Ishimwe Jacqueline (Kampala, Uganda), Pastor MUHINDO BAKULENE(BENI,DRC), Brother MUSUBAO BAHATI (BENI,DRC), MAKELELE ORIGENE(BENI,DRC), Dekila Nzanzu (Beni, DRC), Rev Luvundu Sutira (Kitsumbiro, DRC), Rev MUHINDO MASIMANGO TCHUMA(Director of Oneness Development Institute, Beni, DRC), Bishop Luvao Jerusalem ( the Founder and Leading Pastor of New Life Pentecostal Church International, Beni/DRC), the members of Ebenezer Evangelical Church International (DRC), the international prayer team of the Gospel Faith Messenger and other people who have supported this work spiritually and financially.

My grateful thanks go also to Joan Emery, Gisborne, New Zealand, for the editing of this book.



All Scripture quotations, except those noted otherwise, are from the New International Version (NIV) and some are from Life Application Study Bible (NLT) of the Bible.

**Foreword**

In this book we are challenged to believe the powerful finished work on Calvary by Jesus Christ and the impact that this can have on our lives as we truly believe the words of Jesus. May you be encouraged, stirred and challenged to draw closer to Jesus as you grasp more of the reality of the teachings of the Book of Ephesians. There is so much more to accomplish as we believe the teachings of Jesus today. Well done, Pastor Mahamba Wa-ibera Evariste.

~ ***Rodney W. Francis***

Founder/Director: The Gospel Faith Messenger Ministry (New Zealand)

Website: www.gospel.org.nz

The letter to the Ephesians is a wonderfully concise, yet comprehensive, summary of the Christian good news and its implications. Nobody can read it without being moved to wonder and worship and challenged to live a consistent Christian life. As you read and study this great book by Pastor Mahamba Wa-ibera Evariste , truth will leap out. And "*you shall know the truth, and the truth shall make you free.*" So be careful, get ready, be prepared, because you'll be challenged, changed, transformed, you'll discover who you really are, and you'll find the freedom Jesus offers as you read.

- Stephen Whitwell, New Zealand, www.goodwords.nz

It was with great joy that I began to read even the first chapter of this, Pastor Mahamba Wa-ibera Evariste 's first book. Many will be able to identify with having walked the very road he so accurately describes - but not without redeeming hope. As the Word of God says, "There is a way that seems right to a man, but its end is the way of death" (Proverbs 14:12 NKJV). In the body of the text Pastor Mahamba says, "We should not be committed to accomplishing our will or someone else's will, but we should ask God to reveal to us His will, so that we can be committed to it daily." As Pastor Mahamba Wa-ibera Evariste expands on the significance of the Book of Ephesians, his enthusiasm instills encouragement and hope in the life of every believer who will take hold of his words. In the few years that I have been connected to

Pastor Mahamba Wa-ibera Evariste and his ministry, I have seen him take the Word of the Lord He so loves, put it into practice and then reap the eternal results. His passion for living out the truth of the Word of God in his everyday life whilst disciplining others to do the same is evident to all. May God richly bless and encourage every person who reads this book.
Karen Reid www.lifeministries.org.nz (hello@lifeministries.org.nz)

This book is a very encouraging book, and especially so if you are experiencing hardship in your walk
with Jesus Christ. Pastor Mahamba Wa-ibera Evariste has a solid genuine belief and love for Jesus Christ which shines through his writings. Bless you Pastor Mahamba Wa-ibera Evariste and bless this book. May it touch, encourage and bless many who are seeking to know and understand God's will and purpose for their lives. I pray that it will help many to continue to endure and press forward to reach the goal and get the prize of the high calling of God in Jesus Christ (Philippians 3:14).
Tania Francis
www.christianconnection.co

**Introduction**

Let us first speak about the purpose of the book of Ephesians. Its purpose is to strengthen the believers at Ephesus in their Christian faith by explaining the nature and purpose of the Church, the Body of Christ. So this book of Ephesians has the purpose of strengthening (encouraging) believers of *every* generation in their Christian faith by explaining the nature and purpose of the Church, the Body of Christ.

I have been amazed as I have been reading Ephesians Chapter 1 because God has been revealing Himself to me in a special way, which I will go into in some depth now. In this book I am sharing the insights that God has revealed to me as I have studied His Word. And this, being my first book, I trust that God will enrich abundantly your life as you read every sentence within its pages.

My prayer is that this work may impact thousands of people around the world who are searching for and accomplishing the plans and purposes of God for their lives so they can be successful every day, week, month and year, regardless of the circumstances they are meeting as they walk daily with our Lord Jesus Christ.

We are living in a world in which only few people know the plans and purposes God has for their lives. And many of those who know them are frustrated, as it seems as if their future is dark because of the obstacles they frequently meet along their daily walk as they attempt to move forward. But let us look into the scriptures so that we can see if, in God's plan for people, there can be found a plan for each one of us that can propel us forward, after discovering it to be somewhat frustrating, depressing, and hopeless. I believe that, after reading this book, you will be encouraged as you discover God's plans and purposes for your life, and you will be encouraged to become committed in accomplishing them. Thus, you will live a hopeful life filled with confidence as you go forward with a wonderful plan for your future.

**CONTENTS**

**The Will of God for Your Life - Ephesians 1:1**
**Chapter 1**

The book of Ephesians 1:1 says: "Paul, an apostle of Christ Jesus by the will of God ..." Let us search in the scriptures of the Bible to learn about the life of Saul of Tarsus before he became Paul, the apostle of Christ Jesus.
In our search we see Paul (called Saul) coming into the scene in Acts 7:58: ". . . And dragged him (Stephen) out of the city and began to stone him. Meanwhile the witnesses laid their clothes at the feet of a young man named Saul." If we read from Acts 6:8 to Acts 7:58 we will know the background to verse 58. But let me tell you in short the story of Stephen, who was stoned to death, as this above verse declares, so that we can understand our message. Stephen was a chosen deacon in the first church and he was a man full of God's grace and power; he performed great wonders and amazing miraculous signs among the people. As a result, opposition arose from the synagogue of the Freedmen - Jews of Cyrene and Alexandria, as well as the provinces of Cilicia and Asia. These men began to argue with Stephen but they could not stand up to the wisdom or the Spirit by Whom he spoke. When they became defeated by his speech, they finally decided to stone him outside the town. The clothes of those who witnessed the death of Stephen were then deposited at the feet of Saul, who at that time knew nothing about God's plans and purposes for his life. He was designated to watch over the clothing of those who were stoning Stephen to death.
Let us continue with our message as we read Acts 8:1-3: "And Saul was there, giving approval to his death. On that day a great persecution broke out against the church at Jerusalem, and all except the apostles were scattered throughout Judea and Samaria. Godly men buried Stephen and mourned deeply for him. But Saul began to destroy the church, going from house to house he dragged off men and women and put them in prison." And Saul was there, giving approval to the death of Stephen while he was being killed by stoning. Saul, who knew nothing about the will or plan of God for his life, gave approval to the death of Stephen, the disciple of Jesus Christ. And the Bible tells us that on that day a great persecution broke out against the church at Jerusalem. Those who persecuted the church were the same people who gave approval to Stephen's death by stoning. And they were religious men of the synagogue of the Freedmen. Saul (Paul) was a member of this religious group of people and he joined them in persecuting the Church, resulting in all disciples of Jesus Christ (except the apostles) being scattered throughout Judea and Samaria. Lastly, verse 3 speaks about Saul destroying the Church by going from house to house, dragging out men and women and throwing them into prison. If Saul could have known God's plan for his life when he was still a child he would not have given approval to Stephen's death; he would not have joined those who persecuted and scattered the disciples of Jesus; he would not have carried out his disgraceful behaviour of imprisonment to the Christians. If he knew God's will or plan for his life he could have spared the life of Stephen and learnt much from him. He could instead, as a young man, been mentored by

him and other disciples of Jesus who were around him.

Many people are still destroying the Church today because they are not searching for God's will for their lives. They don't search for God's will or plan for people around them, and they don't ask themselves why God has allowed certain people to be around them. You have to know that there is God's will or plan for everyone who is joining your church, your family, your nation, your organization and/or your group, regardless of their race, sex, social class or ethnic background.

One cannot also rule out the fact that Satan can send people, his 'missionaries' who come with a mission of destroying us: people who are still controlled by him. But God will protect us against any attack from the devil. Remember that God has a plan for even those who are still under the control of the devil; there is God's will for their lives and they are still under His jurisdiction, even though they (and we) have no understanding of it at this point in their lives.

Many leaders, whether in churches or in Christian organizations, are persecuting, scattering and destroying people who could be a great support for their future success, but, because they don't search for God's will for these people whom God has placed around them, they have no vision for them or their future. These leaders discover the will of God for the lives of these people many days, weeks, months or years after scattering and destroying them, as God saves them when they begin to trust in the LORD; God makes them like mountains that cannot be shaken and they endure sufferings without being shaken like mountains. Once they have put their trust in God He surrounds them like the mountains that are surrounding Jerusalem, and as a result no obstacle can shake them as they go forward for God's plans for their lives (Psalm 125:1-2). We praise God, Who is gathering His people who have been scattered by leaders, but who are now growing in the will of God for their lives. The Lord is healing those who have been wounded and hurt by different circumstances; He is turning their weaknesses into strength; He is healing the broken hearts. And people who had broken hearts are becoming spiritually strong as they trust in the LORD.

When someone scatters God's people and hurts them, who is the loser, God or the leader scattering people around him? The leader is the loser because he cannot prosper without the people in God's will or plan that God has placed around him for his success. Whenever people start growing in churches or organizations, many top leaders then use their means of attack to destroy them. But, after destroying them, these leaders always regret their actions when they discover God's will for the people they destroyed. We praise God, Who is able to rebuild a destroyed man or woman and make him/her a strong vessel that can no longer be destroyed by any person or any force.

As we search for scriptures in the Bible, we will find that, although Paul destroyed the Church bought by the blood of Jesus Christ, God restored it, as He was keeping His Word that "the gates of Hell will not overcome it" (Matthew 6:18): "And I tell you the truth that you are Peter, and on this rock (this revelation) I will build My Church, and the gates of Hades will not overcome it." Praise is to God, Who cannot allow whatever that is in His will to be overcome. The Bible says that we, believers of Jesus Christ, are more than conquerors through Jesus Christ Who loved us – Romans 8:37: "No, in all these things (trouble, hardship, persecution, famine, nakedness, danger, or sword (verse35), we are more than conquerors through Him Who loved us."

Before we go further, let us see how obstacles or circumstances cannot hinder God from accomplishing His will in someone's life, but out of these He continues to pursue His will so that He can be victorious as He fulfils His plans. Let us read 2 Corinthians 12:9-10: "But He said to me, 'My grace is sufficient for you, for My power is made perfect in weakness.' Therefore I will boast all the more gladly about my weaknesses, so that Christ's power may rest on me. That is why I delight in weaknesses, in insults, in hardships, in persecutions, in difficulties. For when I am weak, then I am strong."

God's grace is sufficient for us as He is pursuing His will for life even though we may be now in weaknesses, in insults, in hardships, in persecutions, and in difficulties, for God's power is made perfect in such circumstances. So we have to boast as we are passing through these situations because we are expecting to become strong. The apostle Paul says in one of his books: "Not only so, but we also rejoice in our suffering because suffering brings perseverance, perseverance character, and character hope, and hope does not disappoint us..." The Grace of God is able to reach anyone so that God can do anything as He pursues His plans for everyone individually.

As we continue to learn about God's will for Paul's life, let us read Acts 9:1. "Meanwhile, Saul was still breathing out murderous threats against the Lord's disciples. He went to the high priest and asked him for letters to the synagogues in Damascus so that if he found any there who belonged to the way, whether men or women, he might take them as prisoners to Jerusalem."

Paul gave approval to the death of Stephen. He was among those who scattered the Church, destroying it himself, going from house to house to drag out and imprison men and women who were disciples of Jesus Christ. He carried out these offences because he was persecuting the Church, but he was still not satisfied, his results did not have a far-reaching effect; his murderous threats against the Lord's disciples needed to cover a much larger territory. In his great obsession to destroy the Church, he went to the high priest requesting letters to the synagogues in Damascus in order to hunt down more followers of Jesus Christ and take them also as prisoners to Jerusalem. He had great zeal to serve the high priest, thus accomplishing his passion and will to destroy the Church. We should not be committed to accomplishing our own will or someone else's will, but we should ask God to reveal to us His will so that we can be committed to it daily, and if we cannot distinguish between God's will, ours and someone else's, we will be fighting God's will without knowing (as Saul did for so long) and using up all our energy.

No-one is able to fight God's will, knowing or without knowing, and win. As Saul was near Damascus, he met with Jesus Christ Who was ambushing him, and as Saul lost control, he had no choice but to surrender to God's will for his life as it was revealed to him by Jesus Himself, Who met with him on the road to Damascus. Then, as he pursued God's will for his life, he planted many churches, he wrote many books, he strengthened many churches in their faith, he got surpassingly great revelations from God when he reached in the third heaven, and he became the great apostle Paul.

For you and me to know God's will for our life, we have first to respond to the universal invitation of receiving Jesus Christ as our personal Lord and Saviour. We have to know that Jesus Christ died on the cross as our substitute, and we have to know that He took all our sins in His own body. He took also our curses, and He abolished the wall that was separating us from our God, our Creator. He broke into pieces a written document for our condemnation: a document that contained all the details of sins and transgressions. This is a book in which are written all our sins and iniquities, and which Jesus Christ can use whenever He is seated on the judgment seat in condemning any sinner and any transgressor.

As soon as we receive Jesus Christ as Lord and Saviour, we begin a daily walk with Him, which includes meeting with other followers of His, reading and meditating on the Word of God, praying individually and with others as we speak to our Heavenly Father, Who has a wonderful plan for our life. As we will cultivate this style of meeting with other born-again Christians, and as we pray, read and meditate on the Word of God, He will reveal to us His will for our life, and we will surely find it. We will become what God predestined us to be, and if we always do that which God tells us to do, He will accomplish His will and plans for our life as we move with Him in accomplishing His plans for our life.

May you allow me to conclude this chapter as I tell you about the will of God for my life. I am now a Visionary and Senior Pastor of Ebenezer Evangelical Church International. I have a vision of planting churches around the nations of the world as we minister to people who have no hope, and the fear of God is enabling us to do it as we trust God daily to supply all our needs. I first responded to the universal invitation of receiving Jesus Christ as Lord and Saviour, and as I do always what God tells me to do, He always reveals Himself to me through His word as He opens up opportunities, so that I can know His perfect will for my life. I have discovered that I am not only a Senior Pastor but I am also a writer of books and articles. I believe that as I will continue to serve Him faithfully, and as I will continue to do what He tells me to do through His word, regardless of circumstances, He will once again reveal to me His additional will or plans for my life as He speaks to me through His Word and as He opens other opportunities.

**You Are Saints in God's Sight - Ephesians 1:1**
**Chapter 2**

We will always start our chapters with Ephesians Chapter One, and we will always get other scriptures for support from other verses of the Bible. The book of Ephesians was sent to the saints in Ephesus. When we receive Jesus Christ as Lord and Saviour, we become saints in the sight of God as He transfers His holiness and justice in and toward us - we read this in 2 Corinthians 5:17,19 "Therefore, if anyone is in Christ, he is a new creation; the old has gone, the new has come. Verse 19: "Knowing that God was reconciling the world to Himself in Christ, not counting men's sins against them . . ." The Life Application Study Bible (NLT) says: "This means that anyone who belongs to Christ has become a new person; the old life is gone; a new life has begun! Verse 19: "For God was in Christ, reconciling the world to Himself, no longer counting people's sins against them. And He gave us this wonderful message of reconciliation."

When we have not yet received Jesus Christ as Lord and Saviour, we are living an old life that is under the control of sin and dominated by the devil. And that life causes us to live independently from God as we rebel against Him in violating God's holy law, the Holy Scriptures. And then God sees us as dead and without holiness in His sight. But when we receive Jesus Christ as Lord and Saviour, we begin to live a new life as Jesus Christ causes it to ignite and grow within us daily: as we keep trusting Him. Since the time Jesus enters into our life we are no longer living our old life but we start living a new one, and even people around us will discover that there is a new life that Jesus Christ is producing as He causes new things to come from us for both our benefit and the benefit of many people around us. The life Jesus Christ begins within us is a holy life, filled with God's character. And as this new life manifests itself through us, people around us will benefit from it as God fulfils His plans for them through us.

God makes us holy because He is holy. That's why it says in His Word that we have to be holy even as He is holy (1 Peter 1:15-16). Our heavenly Father is holy, and through the process of receiving Jesus Christ as Lord and Saviour, He transforms us into His holy sons and holy daughters. And as He is holy, we become born of Him as holy people like our heavenly Father. So, because we are saints, do we have freedom to sin? And, if we continue sinning as we stop trusting God, will God continue to keep connecting to Himself? No. Let us meditate on the book of Romans 6:8-14 that says: "And since you died with Christ, you know you will also live with Him. We are sure of this because Christ was raised from the dead, and He will never die again. Death no longer has any power over Him. When He died, He died once to break the power of sin. But now that He lives, He lives for the glory of God. So you should consider yourselves dead to the power of sin and alive to God through Christ Jesus. Do not let sin control the way you live. Do not give in to sinful desires. Do not let any part of your body become an instrument of evil to serve sin. Instead, we give ourselves completely to God, for we were dead, but now we have a new life. So we use our whole body as an instrument to do what is right for the glory of God. Sin is no longer our master, for we no longer live under the requirements of the law. Instead we live under the freedom of God's grace."

Let us learn from the following verses the reason why we should continue to keep ourselves holy as we continue trusting God, so that we can continue being connected to Him through Abraham, the father of our faith. As we read carefully the following verses, we will discover God can cut off any branch, any believer who stops trusting God or Jesus Christ to be their Master and Source for his/her provisions, and He can reconnect anyone who comes again to Him after sinning greatly against their Creator.

Turn now to Romans 11:12-24: "Now if the Gentiles were enriched because the people of Israel turned down God's offer of salvation, think how much greater a blessing the world will share when they finally accept it. I am saying all this for you Gentiles. God has appointed me as the apostle to the Gentiles. I stress this, for I want somehow to make the people of Israel jealous of what you Gentiles have, so I might save them. For since their rejection meant that God will offer salvation to the rest of the world, their acceptance will be also even more wonderful. It will be life for those who were dead! And since Abraham and the other patriarchs were holy, their descendants will also be holy - just as the entire batch of dough is holy because the portion given as an offering is holy - for if the roots of the tree are holy, the branches will be also. But some of these branches from Abraham's tree - some of the people of Israel - have been broken off. And you Gentiles, who were branches from a wild olive tree, have been grafted in. So now you also receive the blessing God has promised Abraham and his children, sharing in the rich nourishment from the root of God's special olive tree. But you must not brag about being grafted in to replace the branches that were broken off. You are just a branch, not a root. "Well", you may say, "those branches were broken off to make room for me." Yes, but remember - those branches were broken off because they didn't believe in Christ, and you are there because you do believe. So don't think highly of yourself, but fear what could happen. For if God did not spare the original branches, He won't spare you either. Notice how God is both kind and severe. He is severe to those who disobeyed, but kind to you if you continue to trust in His kindness. But if you stop trusting, you also will be grafted off. And if the people of Israel turn from their unbelief, they will be grafted in again, for God has power to graft back into the tree. You, by nature, were a branch cut from a wild olive tree. So if God was willing to do something contrary to nature by grafting you into His cultivated tree, He will be far more eager to graft the original branches back into the tree where they belong."

I trust that the Holy Spirit has revealed to us much about the above verses. May we continue to keep our holiness as we continue to keep our trust in God. How is our faith today?

**Have in mind that you and I died with Christ when He died on the cross on our behalf as our substitute.**

And if you and I died with Him, we have to remember that we were crucified with Him on the cross. When Jesus Christ was buried He was buried with us, and our sins were deposited in His body. When He rose from the dead, He rose with you and me, as He left our sins forever in the grave. As we rose with Him, we believe that we will live with Him in eternity in His coming kingdom that will endure forever. Because He has made us holy like Himself, and He cannot change His mind or the promises in His Word, He says that no wicked thing will enter His Coming Kingdom. We are no longer wicked people because God has made us saints after cleansing us by the blood of Jesus Christ. We are sure of this because Christ was raised from the dead, and He will never die again. In the same way, anyone who has been made holy by God can never become once again a sinner if they continue to keep trusting God, walking with God, maintaining their holiness, regardless of the unsaved people around them.

**Death no longer has power over Jesus Christ.**

Death has no longer any power over Jesus Christ, Who was raised from the dead. In the same way, sin no longer has power over us who believe in the risen Lord Jesus Christ because when Jesus died He broke the power of sin, and it was broken once for all. Our Lord Jesus is now living for the glory of God, and as He lives for God's glory, we should consider ourselves as dead to the power of sin because our Lord Jesus Christ, Who broke the power of sin once for all is living within our hearts permanently. It is the reason why our verse tells us that: "We do not let sin control the way we live" for our way of living should be controlled by Jesus Christ as we live under the influence of the Holy Spirit, because Jesus Christ has become our Master as soon as we receive Him as Lord and Saviour. The Bible tells us that we do not have to live according to our sinful nature but we have to live according to the Holy Spirit, Whom we receive as soon as we welcome Jesus Christ to enter into us as our Lord and Saviour. He is given to us by God to take His permanent place within us as a seal, which is a sign of our being children of God.

And we are not to let any part of our body become an instrument of evil to serve sin. Every part of our body is sacred and it has its specific purpose that is to be used for every work which is for God's glory. There are born-again Christians who are using their body parts as instruments of evil to serve sin as if they were still under the control of sin. And as a result, they are living fruitless lives as sin destroys daily their spiritual potential. Their prayer becomes powerless, and as they continue sinning, they become like unbelievers who are spiritually dead.

Dear brothers and sisters, a Christian life is a life that has to be maintained as we walk daily with God: as we maintain our holiness: as we continue trusting God. To maintain our holiness means that we have to continue doing what God tells us to do, and if we do not do it, we have to know that we are sinning against God. Many born-again Christians are sinning against God because they are not giving themselves completely to God. Our God wants to have children who give themselves to Him, regardless of obstacles and hardships they meet in their daily walk with Jesus.

We should also choose friends who are using their whole body as an instrument that does all for the glory of God. Do you know that our friends influence us in their words and actions? There are also those ministers who are teaching the wrong message, which is encouraging the hearers to sin: like ministers who are committing adultery with church members as they deceive them, saying that one can fornicate or commit adultery with them because they are chosen by God and they have a covenant with God. So they can ask God for their forgiveness and then ask forgiveness for church members who are sinning with them as soon as they complete their evil act of sexual immorality.

Read the Word of God daily and also meditate on it. Search the Scriptures, like the Berean people (Acts 17:10-11), who were searching the Scriptures to know if what they were being taught was biblical or not. As we know the truth, no-one can deceive us if they give a wrong interpretation of the Word of God. We are to maintain our holiness, being aware that Satan is doing his best to cause us to sin. "Resist the devil and he will flee from you" (James 4:7). Yes, we must resist him because sin is no longer our master, for we no longer live under the requirements of the Law. Instead we live under the freedom of God's grace. That enables you and me to live as a free man or woman in Christ as we continue to live a holy life. Living under the freedom of God's grace is a wonderful assurance for those who are saints in God's sight, because if we are saints in God's sight by grace, we have to know that God will continue to keep us daily and this will enable us to live in the Spirit of God, as it is written below in the verses of Romans 8:1-17.

**"So now there is no condemnation for those who belong to Christ Jesus" - Romans 8:1.**

We don't have to condemn ourselves if we feel as if we are not a saint in the Lord's sight because we already belong to Jesus Christ after receiving Him as Lord and Saviour.

**"The power of the life-giving Spirit has freed those who belong to Christ Jesus from the power of sin that leads to death" - Romans 8:2.**

We have to know that the indwelling Holy Spirit is a life-giving Spirit, Who has all power to give us life. He has freed or set us free from the power of sin that leads to death. Sin is not to be taken for granted because it leads to death. Satan is a killer and he knows that the only method he can use as he destroys us is to cause us to sin, because he knows that sin leads to spiritual, even physical death.

I remember my best friend, whom God was using mightily, when he fell from grace and started fornicating. We advised him many times to stop such evil deeds but he would not listen to us. As he became more entrenched in fornication, he fell sick and died after some months. Praise God that he repented publically in our prayer service before he died. However, the consequence of his fornication was to impregnate someone else's wife, leaving her child fatherless because my friend died before the birth of the baby. The woman also went through consequences that I cannot go into, but as she was also about to die under the judgment of God, she repented, and the burning anger of God was halted. A tree fell on the child and he died also when he was about three years old. I am reminding us all that sin leads to death and no-one wants to die prematurely. So let us not tolerate sin or be under its control. Let us be always flexible to the Holy Spirit as we have learnt in this verse that He is a life-giving Spirit, Who is powerful.

**The Law of Moses was unable to save us because of the weakness of our sinful nature Romans 8:3.**

There are ten commandments in the Bible that we find in the book of Exodus Chapter 20 and these commandments were summarized by Jesus Christ in these terms: "Love God with all your soul, with all your mind, with all your strength and love your neighbour as yourself." But there are many laws which Moses wrote in his five books - Genesis, Exodus, Leviticus, Numbers and Deuteronomy. These Books of Moses are called the Law of Moses, and as we pass through these books we discover they are filled with many laws given by God through Moses.

The laws written in these five Books of Moses were unable to save us because of the weakness of our sinful nature. Likewise, there are often laws given to many church members and many people who want to become born-again Christians or who are already born-again Christians. But we have to know that the Law of Moses or the laws made by some of today's religious leaders are unable to save us because of the weakness of our sinful nature. Our sinful nature is very weak so it is not able to accomplish or live according to the Law of Moses, including the Ten Commandments, and the laws given by religious leaders. We may start living by these laws but, because of the weakness of our sinful nature, we will fail to live as these laws require. Finally we will be seen living as a hypocrite, pretending to live according to the requirements of the law, although not fully keeping them. And, even if we lived according to the law, we cannot please God nor can we be justified by our good works; God cannot write our name in the Book of Eternal Life because we are living according to the requirements of the law. But He will justify us because of our faith in the Lord Jesus Christ, Who died as our substitute on the cross. And, after receiving Jesus Christ as Lord and Saviour, we have to live according to the guidance of the Word of God, because He has made us a new creation, flexible to His leadership.

**So God did what the Law could not do - Romans 8:3.**

The law could not forgive a sinner like you and me. It could not forgive a condemned person because it was a "pay-back" system, paying everyone according to his/her deeds . . . "tooth was for tooth and eye was for eye" (Exodus 21:24 & Leviticus 24:20). People were being punished according to what they had done.

But God loved us when we were still sinners, when we were still under the curse, and He sent Jesus Christ to die on the cross as our substitution, dying like a criminal. He sent His own Son in a body, just like the bodies we sinners have. And in that body God declared an end to sin's control over us by giving His Son as a sacrifice for our sins. He purchased us with His own blood and He made us His people, He forgave us, He justified us, He made us His children, He put us in His Son Jesus Christ, He deposited His Holy Spirit within us . . . and He wrote our names in the Book of Life because there is no longer condemnation for those who are in Christ Jesus. So God did what the law could not do, and He is still doing what the law cannot do, and He is still doing what religious leaders cannot do if they apply the law in churches and Christian organizations. God is restoring backsliders. He is raising up mighty servants of God who were once rejected and regarded as disqualified, according to the law of their churches and Christian organizations.

**We are no longer following our sinful nature but instead we are following the Spirit Romans 8:4.**

Have we abandoned following our sinful nature? If our answer is 'yes', praise the Lord for that because this will mean we are following the Spirit. The Holy Spirit knows every detail of God's will or plan for our life. If God deposited Him within us, it is because God wants us to follow the Holy Spirit as He guides us in fulfilling His will or plan for our life. Jesus says that His Word is "life and Spirit." As we hear the Word of God and live according to it, we are following the Spirit. To those "in the world", following the Spirit is like following the wind. The wind blows wherever it wants. Just as we can hear the wind but can't tell where it comes from or where it is going, so we can't explain how people are born of the Spirit John 3:8. We can't even explain how and why people follow the Spirit but we always see the amazing results of their obedience to the Spirit and the Word of God.

**Those who are dominated by the sinful nature think about sinful things - Romans 8:5.**

Before we became born-again Christians we were dominated by our sinful nature and we thought about sinful things. The Bible says that everyone was following their own way of sinning; our thoughts were dominated by sinful things that were expressed in our speech and actions. But now, by the grace of God, we are no longer dominated by our sinful nature; we are no longer thinking sinful things; but we think heavenly things as we receive them daily through the Word of God.

**But those who are controlled by the Holy Spirit think about things that please the Spirit Romans 8:5.**

Are we really thinking about things that please the Spirit? Maybe, because we are going to weekly church services, we think this is a sign that we are thinking about the things that please the Spirit. Maybe we are giving our regular tithe and offerings? Maybe we have a high position in our church or our Christian organization? Maybe we are a pastor of a big church? But, all the above deeds are only a portion of things we are thinking about so we can please the Holy Spirit. We should let the Holy Spirit control us completely, and once we are controlled by Him, we will always think about things that please and glorify Him.

**A mind controlled by sinful nature is heading towards death - Romans 8:6.**
This world is filled with things, programs and products that Satan is using in his efforts to lure us once again to be controlled by sinful natures that lead to death. Keeping our mind in the control of the Holy Spirit has a goal of giving us life as we allow God's Word to control our mind. So we have to choose spiritual friends, songs that uplift our spirit, Christian books that build our faith, and TV programs without profanity. In this manner we can keep our mind controlled by the Holy Spirit because letting the Spirit control our mind leads to life and peace.
**The sinful nature is hostile to God. It never did obey God's laws, and it never will Romans 8:7.**
A person who has a mind controlled by sinful nature is hostile to God. Can we think about the result of our being hostile to God? Imagine now the end result of those who are becoming hostile to God as they fight and oppose Him by their words and actions. To the many rebels and leaders in our countries who have become hostile, they should recognize the fact that the end result has never been favorable or positive.

**Satan never did obey God's laws.**

The sinful nature is a nature programmed by Satan in the Garden of Eden through Adam and Eve, our grandparents. It was programmed for disobeying God's laws, as we have seen as we read the history of people who lived during different generations. But people who allowed God to re-program their mind were obeying God's laws, and God's laws will continue to be obeyed today by those who will allow Him to reprogram their mind, because He has programmed them for obedience to His laws before the foundation of the world.

**Fallen nature will never obey God's laws.**

Right now, we are living with people who are not obeying the laws (Word) of God because they are not allowing God's Word to control their mind. Even in the future, those who will not allow God's Word to control their mind will never obey God's laws (Word).
**Those who are still under the control of their sinful nature can never please God Romans 8:8.**
The God, Whom we are not pleasing if we live under the control of our sinful nature, has provided for us the Holy Spirit, Who can enable us to please Him. Let us remember there is no reason to remain under the control of our sinful nature but every reason to be obedient to God. These verses from the book of Romans 8:9-10 says: "You are controlled by the Spirit if you have the Spirit living in you. And remember that those who do not have the Spirit of Christ living in them do not belong to Him at all."
To be controlled by the Spirit means: *to be influenced by the Holy Spirit; to be obedient to*

*the Word of God; to accept the leadership of Holy Spirit.* We may claim that we belong to Christ but if we are not allowing the Spirit of God to control us, we have to know that we do not belong to Christ at all. Or we belong to Christ but still lack the teaching about the role of the Holy Spirit within our lives. But, those who are controlled by the Holy Spirit belong to Christ.

**And Christ lives within you, so even though your body will die because of sin, the Spirit gives you life because you have been made right with God - Romans 8:10.**

As Jesus Christ lives within us, we believe that the Holy Spirit will continue to give us spiritual life while we live here on the earth because we have been made right with God, even though our bodies will die because of sin.

**The Spirit of God, Who raised Christ Jesus from the dead, lives in you - Romans 8:11.**

Just as God raised Christ from the dead, He will give life to our mortal bodies by this same Holy Spirit living within us. The Holy Spirit is able to give divine life to our mortal bodies, and He can also enable us to live a holy life although our bodies are weak. Our body is mortal because it still has sinful desires which can lead us to death if we live according to them. But the Holy Spirit living within us gives always divine life to our bodies so that we can overcome and conquer the sinful nature, allowing the Holy Spirit to control us. We have to remember this Spirit of God, Who lives within us, is a Holy Spirit Who is Almighty. As He used His power to raise Christ Jesus from the dead, He still has that mighty power, which He uses as He enables us to live and maintain a holy life.

The Holy Spirit is living permanently within us to work on our holiness as we live here on earth. So we should always be flexible to His control because He is the One Who knows which direction we can take. As God sees that His Holy Spirit is living within us, He sees us as saints. Because we are saints in God's sight, we should always pray God to enable us always to be saint-like people for the glory of God.

**We have no obligation to do what our sinful nature urges us to do - Romans 8:12.**

One may say that the sinful nature always comes to us powerfully, asking us to do what it desires. But we have to know that the Holy Spirit is more powerful than the sinful nature. It is the reason why this verse is telling us, "You have no obligation to do what your sinful nature asks you to do, but you have obligation to do what the Holy Spirit tells you to do because this is for your benefit of giving and for the benefit of people around you." Therefore, if we live by the dictates of our sinful nature, we will die. But if we live through the power of the Holy Spirit that put to death our sinful deeds, we will live, and many people around us will also have spiritual life through our testimony.

**For all who are led by the Spirit of God are children of God - Romans 8:14-15.**

If we are children of God, we should also be under the leadership of the Holy Spirit because this will approve that we are children of God when we allow the Holy Spirit to lead us. Do you know that being led by the Spirit is one of the reasons why God sent Him to come and live within us? Let us read John 16:13: "When the Spirit of truth comes, He will guide you into all truth." The Holy Spirit is the One Who knows all truth and the truth is Jesus Christ. It means that the Holy Spirit will lead us to the full knowledge of Jesus Christ. To know Him as the Saviour of the world is not enough - we should know Him fully. We should always allow the Holy Spirit to guide us into all truth, and this truth, Jesus Christ, will enable us to live a holy life that pleases God. And God will be praised as we live a holy life among wicked people.

We have not received a Spirit that makes us slaves. Instead, we received God's Spirit when He adopted us as His own children. Now we can call Him, "Abba, Father." And, become a Holy God is the One Who has adopted us, He cannot call us His son if He has not made us a saint like Him. It is the reason why He is allowing us to call Him 'Father': the S*aint Father* Who has *saint children.* See yourself as saint because the Saint God has adopted you as His own son.

**For His Spirit joins our spirit to affirm that we are God's children - Romans 8:16-17.**

God's Spirit joins our spirit as soon as we receive Jesus Christ as Lord and Saviour. And we have to remember that this is a Holy Spirit, Who joins our spirit to make us a *saint son or saint daughter of God.* And, because we are God's *saint children,* we are His heirs. In fact, together with Christ, we are heirs of God's glory. But if we are to share His glory, we, His *saint children*, are to share also His suffering.

So, *saint children of God* can suffer also for God's sake, but our suffering doesn't have to push us or cause us to live like children of the darkness, the faithful of Satan. Even in the time of our suffering we should maintain our holiness, just as Jesus Christ did when He suffered and was tempted but did not sin.

**Are you faithful in Christ Jesus? - Ephesians 1:1**
**Chapter 3**

The apostle Paul addressed this letter to the faithful church of Ephesus, the Body of Christ. The members of the church of Ephesus were faithful church members, and, when Paul heard about their faithfulness, he took the opportunity to encourage them when he penned this letter. We don't have the total number of the members of this church, but there is something very important that we have to learn from the members of this church. And what we learn about them is a whole church that was faithful; every church member was faithful in Christ Jesus.

Our God is a faithful God and it is His joy to see that the whole church, the Body of Christ, is a fully functioning faithful church. Let us focus on the local church if it becomes a faithful church. There can be a supernatural result in the church if every church member would become a faithful member. May we remember that God's plan for every born-again Christian is to become faithful in Jesus Christ. Can we comprehend the results of what we are doing for Christ's sake if every church member could be faithful to do everything the Lord Jesus Christ tells them to do in a committed way? Our faithful God wants us to do whatever He tells us to do in a committed way, regardless of the obstacles, hardships, sufferings, poverty, nakedness, hunger, and every circumstance we can meet in life.

As we pursue God's will for our life in our local church, we must know that the God Who has appointed us in that church is a faithful God Who expects us to be a faithful servant. And as soon as we become faithful in whatever God is telling us to do for our growth and the growth of our church, God will rely on us because we have become faithful like our Father God is. But if the whole church is a faithful church, God will rely on the whole church because God wants to encompass and use all faithful people. He will always use faithful vessels. So He will use supernaturally every individual of every local church if everyone is faithful. And as a result God will bless supernaturally every member of our local churches.

God planned and purposed you and me to be a faithful servant as we serve Him and as we live our daily walk with the Lord Jesus Christ. Numerous people who are now attending churches and serving in Christian organizations are no longer faithful servants of God because of many reasons. But, their reasons should not have any influence on us; we should attend church meetings faithfully and serve our Mighty God faithfully regardless of the circumstances we meet in life. Do you have a reason that can stop you from serving God faithfully? Do I?

Let us look at some examples of people just like us who served God faithfully, regardless of the obstacles and circumstances.

**Noah**

Genesis 6:5-8: "The LORD saw how great man's wickedness on the earth had become, and that every inclination of the thoughts of his heart was only evil all the time. The LORD was grieved that He had made man on earth, and His heart was filled with pain. So the LORD said, 'I will wipe mankind, whom I have created, from the face of the earth - men and animals, and creatures that move along the ground, and birds of the air - for I am grieved that I have made them.' But Noah found favour in the eyes of the LORD."

Noah was found to be a faithful man to God, regardless of the increased wickedness that was on the earth. We are living today in a world where there is an increase of wickedness, but we should continue to be faithful to God, regardless of the increased wickedness around us. And we have to know that God is still faithful; He will continue to be faithful forever, so He expects us to be faithful like Him, regardless of the circumstances we meet in our lives.

There was great immorality and wickedness on the earth during Noah's generation, and now, as prophesied for these last days, the condition of mankind will be no different. Jesus Christ said in Matthew 24:12-13: "Because of the increase of the wickedness, the love of many people will grow cold, but he who stands firm to the end will be saved." I beg you to read the whole chapter, beginning from verse one to the last verse.

Let us be alert to the increase of wickedness now flooding the world as in the time of Noah. Don't allow this prophecy of 'the love of many people growing cold' to be fulfilled in our life. Even if the love for God of many people may grow cold because of the increase in wickedness, we must stand firm, as our love for God increases daily. Don't allow coldness and hardness of heart to creep in.

**Elijah**

There was a man in Israel called Elijah. As he continued to maintain his faithfulness, ministering to people who had abandoned God to serve idols, finally his faithfulness brought a wonderful result; the whole nation started once again to worship the true and living God of Israel.

1 Kings 18:39: "When all the people saw this, they fell prostrate and cried, "The LORD - He is God! The LORD - He is God."

People around us observe our faithfulness, and although we may not immediately see the wonderful results of our faithfulness, they will soon say like the people of Israel that, "Your God is the LORD," as they acknowledge the results of our faithfulness.

Brothers and sisters, as we serve God and people faithfully in our communities, all the people will discover that the God we serve is the LORD, and as they discover that He is the LORD of faithful people, they will come to Him and become His faithful followers. Our being faithful to God and people is a powerful tool that we born-again Christians have to know to use, but it requires endurance. If we are faithful to God and people, people will put their confidence in us, and they will be attracted to belong to a church of faithful people. But people will flee from churches if they discover that their leaders are not faithful to God and to people. If the whole church of Ephesus was a faithful church, it means that our local church too can be a faithful church if we decide to develop a lifestyle of always being faithful to God and to people. God uses powerfully faithful people, and He gives them a supernatural reward. Elijah was swept up into heaven, carried miraculously to his eternal reward without experiencing death. All the great saints of God in the Bible, from Genesis to Revelation, were faithful men and women who served God and people. And God is expecting every born-again Christian to be faithful to Him and to people, so that the glory can be to God as the result of the service we are doing.

Because we are informed, we don't have to be among the large group of people who will let their love for God become cold. We must continue to maintain our faithfulness because the Bible tells us that "He who stands firm to the end will be saved." To be saved at the end is the payment to our being faithful.

So God is calling every follower of Jesus Christ to be faithful to Him, regardless of the increase of wickedness and trying circumstances met in our daily walk with Him. And as we continue to stand firm, our God will save us; He will welcome us to enter into His banquet, and we will rejoice with Him as He says to us: "Well done, good and faithful servant." Just as Noah and Elijah were faithful to God in times of wickedness, so we should be faithful to our God at all times.

**You Are Blessed By God With Every Blessing In Christ – Ephesians 1:3**
**Chapter 4**

Let us read Ephesians 1:3: "Praise be to the God and Father of our Lord Jesus Christ, Who has blessed us in the heavenly realms with every spiritual blessing in Christ."
Our blessings are in Christ Jesus as our heavenly Father purposed them in Him before the foundation of the world. To have access to them, we have to first respond to the universal invitation of receiving Jesus as Lord and Saviour. There are blessings for every person that God has placed in Christ, and as soon as we receive Jesus Christ as Lord and Saviour we begin to receive them one by one.
Let us list some of these blessings:

1. Salvation from the power of sin and the slavery of Satan. As soon as we get salvation we receive a new life. We become a new creature. God makes us new as He makes all things new for us (2 Corinthians 5:17).
2. Jesus Christ enters the life of everyone who opens the door of their heart for Him (Revelation 3:20).
3. As soon as Jesus Christ enters in our heart, He promises that: "Surely I am with you always, to the end of the age" (Matthew 28:20). Remember that Jesus Christ will always keep His promise of being with us wherever we go because He is faithful.
4. We become justified (to declare free from guilt and shame) and He takes away our curses.
5. We become a child of God.
6. We are made holy.
7. We are a chosen people, a royal priesthood, a holy nation, a people belonging to God (1 Peter 2:9).
8. We are purposed by God in Christ to declare the praises of God, Who called us out of darkness into His wonderful light (1 Peter 2:9).
9. We have eternal life (John 3:16) and pass immediately from death to life.
10. Our name is blotted out of the book of death and God writes it in the Book of Life.
11. We receive the Holy Spirit as a seal, approving that we are a child of God.
12. We receive many other blessings in Christ as we seek God daily and as we walk daily in obedience to the Word the God. We discover these blessings one by one, both as we seek Him individually and as we are taught the teachings of the Bible during our Christian meetings.

Be encouraged to search the Scriptures always, and as we become committed to do whatever God tells us to do, He will always reveal in full every blessing He has for us in Christ Jesus. He will open to us opportunities as He rewards us for being obedient to Him. Because our blessings are in Christ Jesus, so Jesus Christ has to be our Master so that these blessings can be available to us.

**You Were Chosen By God Before The Foundation Of The World Ephesians 1:4**
**Chapter 5**

The message of this chapter is found in Ephesians 1:4: "For He chose us in Him before the creation of the world to be holy and blameless in His sight in love."
Before God made the world, He loved us and chose us in Christ to be holy and faultless in His sight. Let us think carefully about being chosen by God before the foundation of the world. Were only some people chosen by God before the foundation of the world to be holy and faultless? The answer is no. As we read Genesis 1:27: "So God created man in His own image, in the image of God He created him: male and female He created them. God blessed them and said to them, 'Be fruitful and increase in number; fill the earth and subdue it. Rule over the fish of the sea and the birds of the air and over every living creature that moves on the ground.'"
God created man; male and female in His own image, and we have to know that every human being was included in the first man God created in His own image. You and I were also created in the image of God, and because we were created in the image of God, God saw every human being who would be born as holy and blameless in His sight, according to the plan He made for us before the foundation of the world.
Our God is omniscient; He knows everything. As He planned and purposed you and me to be holy and blameless in His sight, He saw also that Satan too had a plan: a plan to destroy God's people from becoming holy and blameless. It is the reason why God prepared two men: the first Adam and the second Adam, so that if the first Adam could be deceived by Satan and contribute to the destruction of God's plan, the second Adam, Jesus Christ, had and always will have the power to restore it.
The first Adam is the first man God created in His own image, and when he was lured by Satan to disobey God and eat the forbidden fruit, his sin was laid upon every future human being so that we automatically lost our holy and faultless status in God's sight. As Adam was sinning in disobeying God, we all sinned in him and therefore fall short from the glory of God.
Before the foundation of the world every human being had an input from the first Adamman created in the Garden of Eden - but he also had an input in the second Adam, Jesus Christ. God was expecting these two Adams to do whatever He instructed them so they could fulfil His plan of producing people who are holy and blameless. The reason why God prepared two men through whom He wanted to produce His holy and blameless people was, if the first man failed to produce the original purposes of God because of his disobedience, the second Adam, Jesus Christ, will accomplish them because He always does whatever God tells Him from the beginning of time.
Adam failed because of disobeying whatever God wanted him to do to produce the holy and blameless people God wanted to have. But Jesus Christ reached God's goal because He did whatever God told Him to do, thus He brought to God a holy and blameless outcome, those

who believed in Him.
Let us read Philippians 2:5-11: "Your attitude should be the same as that of Christ Jesus, Who, being in very nature a God, did not consider equality with God something to be grasped, but He made Himself nothing, taking the very nature of a servant, being made in human likeness. And being found in appearances as a man, He humbled Himself and became obedient to death - even death on the cross. Therefore God exalted Him to the highest place and gave Him the name that is above every name, that at the name of Jesus every knee should bow, in heaven and on earth and under the earth, and every tongue confess that Jesus Christ is Lord, to the glory of God the Father."
Let me remind you again of the title of this book, *God's Plans And Purposes For Your Life,* as
we apply these verses to our lives, giving attention to the complete obedience of the second Adam, Jesus Christ.

**The attitude of Jesus Christ - Philippians 2:5.**

God prepared two men so that He could produce through them holy and blameless people in His sight. In the same way, God prepared many people around the world and in every generation who will accomplish His plans here on earth, including you and me. And we are called to do whatever He tells us to do, regardless of the obstacles and circumstances we meet within our daily living. As soon as God chooses to work with us as He accomplishes His plans for the world, the nations, families and individual lives, He will work with us, regardless of our age, race or gender when we begin to develop a lifestyle of obedience to God, doing whatever He tells us to do. God does not want to hear excuses from people He is aiming to work with to accomplish His plans. But rather we have only to trust Him as we put our faith in Him. Let us illustrate this by the example of the first and the second Adam. When the first Adam, man, created in God's image, chose not to obey what God told him to do, the second Adam, Jesus Christ, had immediately an attitude that would enable Him to fulfil the plans of God for humanity. Like Adam, many people are now choosing to follow in his disobedient footsteps, not taking heed to God's Word, but they have to know that God will soon forsake working with those who are choosing this pathway. God's plans will continue to be fulfilled around the world, in the nations, families and lives of those who faithfully adhere to do whatever He tells them to do.
Let us read Matthew 24:45-51: "Who is the faithful and wise servant, whom the master has put in charge of the servants in His household to give them their food at the proper time? It will be good for that servant whose master finds him doing so when He returns. I tell you the truth; He will put him in charge of all His possessions. But suppose that servant is wicked and says to himself, 'My master is staying away a long time,' and then begins to beat his fellow-servants and to eat and drink with drunkards. The master of that servant will come on a day when he does not expect Him and an hour he is not aware of. He will cut him to pieces and assign him a place with the hypocrites, where there will be weeping and gnashing of teeth."

Are we faithful and wise servants of God, so that God can put us in charge of all His possessions (promoting us in our spiritual life) as we do whatever God tells us to do in the proper time? Or are we that wicked one who is beating his servants, and eating and drinking with drunkards because we think that our Lord Jesus Christ is not supervising us? We have to know that our Lord Jesus Christ is the supervisor of everybody, and He rewards everyone according to their deeds done in the proper time, fixed by God.

I remember one day, three years ago, when we were evaluating the work we were doing with some servants of God, and when I reported that we had done nothing for the last month, their attitude was so casual . . . "That's okay, as long as we have breath there's time to get it done!" But we should know that there is a time for every activity under the sun, as it was planned by God before the foundation of the world. We have to respond positively to every Word that comes from the mouth of God. And as we respond to it, we will be doing what God tells us to do in the proper time.

As we have learned about God's plan for our life to be holy and blameless in His sight, do we know what our attitude is to His plans? Are we ready to respond to the universal invitation of receiving Jesus Christ as Lord and Saviour? If our answer is 'yes' then let us pray this prayer:

*Thank You God because You know the plans You have for my life. Thank You for sending Jesus Christ to die on the cross as my substitute. Jesus, I open the door of my heart and I invite You to enter into my life. Forgive me of my sins and wash me clean. In Jesus' name. Amen.*

Be encouraged to join a Christian church so that you can be always equipped, learning much during the teaching of the Word of God in church services. If we are already a born-again Christian, what attitude do we take now as we continue to develop the attitude Jesus Christ had as He was accomplishing God's plans? Receiving Jesus as Lord and Saviour has its precious meaning to God if we continue to maintain being holy and blameless in His sight, doing whatever He tells us to do in a committed way and in the proper time.

**Though Jesus Christ was God, He did not think of equality with God as something to cling**
**to - Philippians 2:6.**

Jesus Christ was God. Jesus Christ is God. His equality with Father God did not prevent Him from having a right attitude (He became slave and human) that enabled Him to accomplish the perfect plan of God for His life. What do we cling to that can hinder us from accomplishing the perfect plan of God for our life as we work in partnership with Him? Whatever we are clinging to is of far less value than the plans God has for our life. But if we do whatever God tells us to do in a committed way and in the proper time, as He pursues fulfilling His plans for our life, we will be amazed to see the hidden potential that lies within each one of us.

In today's society Satan is blinding many people to cling to lesser things and lesser positions, believing they have what is sufficient for their future. But we need to be reminded that the only thing or position we have to cling to that brings a wonderful result is "doing whatever God tells us to do in a committed way and in the proper time made by God Himself as soon as He speaks to us through His Word." Many born-again Christians are no longer being committed to developing their ministries and spiritual gifts because Satan is deceiving them into believing they can be successful without being committed to God's work. Satan deceives when he tells us that God's work does not have to come first, but can be accomplished after we have done what we think is important and useful for us. But God wants to remind us that, as we develop and use our spiritual gifts, He will open opportunities for us which will lead to His plans for our life. We grow more spiritual daily as we become committed to doing whatever God tells us to do. Don't be counted among those church attendees whom Satan is using to discourage others who are committed in serving God, and who are doing what God tells them to do in the proper time. The devil, being 'the king of deception', is more than qualified to cause some Christians to take a wrong road that will lead them to poverty. But God is encouraging those who are committed to serve Him in a committed way, because our reward is great in heaven; God is not unjust and He cannot and will not forget what we are doing.

Satan deceives mankind through their thoughts and circumstances that there is no bright future life for those who are serving God in a committed way, doing whatever God tells them to do in the proper time. He is a champion at glamorizing the attractions in the world to distract us from walking on the narrow path that leads to eternal life. But we should know that we have to do whatever God tells us to do in a committed way, and we have to do it in the proper time, including our involvement and works for our own business. And as we do this, we will be successful in whatever we do, because we are not throwing "the way, the truth and the life" (John 14:6), Jesus Christ, to the ground (see also Daniel 8:12).

Born-again Christian, do not allow job promotions and work positions to cause us to neglect developing and using our spiritual gifts, which I consider as personnel tools that push God to open for us opportunities that lead us to find God's additional plans for our lives. Daniel, who, when promoted to serving in the government, continued developing and using his prophetic gifts. Consequently, he rose above every king who reigned in Babylon, and, when in their jealous anger they had Daniel thrown into the lions' den, Almighty God shut the mouths of the ferocious animals to protect the life of his faithful servant. The devil was whipped and people of all languages worshipped the God of Daniel.

Life will always present us with problems that it seems no-one can solve - problems in our nations, our cities, our churches, our businesses, our families, our own personal lives, etc. We often attribute their source to Satan, or the people around us, or our parents who we felt never prepared wisely for our future. But we overlook the fact that God is able to change any situation if we will always do whatever He tells us to do, using the tools, our spiritual gifts that He has given to us so that He can open up opportunities that will make us strong as we live God's wonderful plan for our lives. These tools are our developed spiritual gifts, which we are using in a committed way and at the proper time. A good example of the negative and positive of this is of the first Adam and the second Adam, Jesus. The first Adam was the major source to his own problems and so he was also source to the problems of all future human beings because he did not do whatever God told him to do. In

the same way, through disobedience, many of God's people throughout the world are the major source of their own problems, which are often without solutions.
But Jesus Christ, the second Adam, did whatever God told Him to do in a committed way, and He did it in the proper time, thus becoming the major source of His exaltation.
And all people who believe in Him, as we do whatever He tells us to do in a committed way and at the proper time, are becoming the source of amazing blessings.
In Beni, the eastern Democratic Republic of Congo, where we are now living since April 2010 till now, our fields have been occupied by rebels who kill civilians with axes, machetes and knives. The death toll in Beni town and Beni territory during this time has risen to more than 400 people, with more than 350 having been kidnapped by those who might be ADF/NALU, Ugandan rebels who tragically are supported by people from different
27
countries. In Beni town on January 2nd, 2014, they killed the commando, Mamadou Ndala Mustafa, as he was heading to completely destroy more rebels, after having defeated the rebels of M23 in Rutsuru. And now, north of Beni, on May 5th, 2015, those who might be the same rebels have started killing also our soldiers and United Nations soldiers from Tanzania. When we count the people who have been killed in the eastern Democratic Republic of Congo since 1994 up till now, the number is above that of those who died during the genocide of Rwanda. And I will not go into the details of what has transpired during these times of the wars, as rebel leaders are being born every year in Eastern Democratic Republic of Congo who are contributing to the destruction of the Democratic Republic of Congo at every level.
But, as we are doing whatever God tells us to do through His Word in a committed way and in the proper time regardless of these sufferings, God is providing for our daily needs as He moves in His mysterious ways. He is caring for people who have no access to their unreachable fields, which are filled with everything needed for their daily living.

**Jesus Christ gave up His divine privileges, taking the humble position of a slave, and that**
**of being born as a human being - Philippians 2:7.**

Taking a humble position is a very important attitude that we can learn from Jesus Christ as we focus on accomplishing God's plans for our lives as we work in partnership with Him. Dear brothers and sisters in the Lord, we were chosen by God before the foundation of the world to be simple and humble, regardless of our education, our position, our wealth, race, and gender. May we always be mindful that God is the One Who enables us to accomplish what we are accomplishing, regardless of our education, wealth, race, gender and/or occupational positions. Some of the disciples of Jesus were uneducated people, but as they became committed in learning from Jesus Christ, they became wiser than those scribes and teachers of the law who were doctors in theology – like Nicodemus. So we should add to our education the teaching of Jesus Christ, which makes us wiser than we naturally are when we take heed to it. God opposes the proud but He gives grace to the humble (James 4:6) . . . pride precedes the fall, but humility precedes the glory.

As we read Philippians 2:5-11 we learn that Jesus Christ humbled Himself in obedience to God and died a criminal's death on the cross. Jesus Christ knew that God's plans for His life was to die a criminal's death on the cross as our substitute, and after that death, God would raise Him from the dead; He would be exalted to the highest place and given the name which is above every name: that at the name of Jesus every knee should bow, in heaven, on earth, and under the earth, and every tongue confess that Jesus Christ is Lord, to the glory of God the Father.

Did God choose us to die a criminal's death like Jesus Christ? No. That is not the plans God has for you and me. But He will allow you and me to pass through difficult situations which He will turn for our good (Romans 8:28). And let us say, like King David, knowing that, even though we pass through the darkest circumstances, we have not to fear any evil because God is beside us, comforting us through His Word (Psalm 23).

Let us read Jeremiah 29:11: "For I know the plans I have for you, says the LORD. They are plans for good and not for disaster, to give you a future and a hope." God knows the plans He has for every human being, and these plans are good. They are not for disaster but they are plans to give us a future and a hope. These plans were made and deposited in Jesus Christ. As soon as we receive Him as Lord and Saviour, He begins to work out these plans because He knows every detail about them. And immediately after receiving Jesus Christ as Lord and Saviour, we receive the Holy Spirit Who knows also every detail about these plans. As we hear God's Word that instructs us, the Holy Spirit enables us to accomplish what God wants us to do. And if we forget to do it, He reminds us of it. When we become committed in doing it in a committed way and in the proper time made by God for every activity under the sun (Ecclesiastes 3) the LORD will accomplish His good plans for us that will give us a future and a hope.

I shared with the servant of God, Rodney W. Francis (who is fully committed to obeying the Lord) that our government had planned to close churches and Christian organizations that have not yet registered with them because some church leaders became rebel leaders in the Democratic Republic of Congo and he told me that I had reminded him of what the Holy Spirit told him when he was in Nairobi, Kenya, saying that the doors of nations are being closed because people are rejecting Jesus Christ. Let us ponder these words in saying that the plans God has for nations, families and human beings are becoming disastrous as people reject Jesus Christ. What about God's plans for your life ... for my life? When we choose to follow and not reject Jesus Christ, God's plans for our life will give us a future and a hope. Rejecting Jesus Christ means not giving Him the place of becoming our Master, thus not doing whatever God tells us to do through His Word: trampling underfoot the precious truth as found in the Gospel of Jesus Christ. Jesus Christ is the Word of God (John 1:1 & 14). And that same Word of God is powerful, able to accomplish every plan God has predestined. So let us continue to give Jesus Christ first place in our life, allowing Him to give us a future and a hopeful life. Jesus Christ, our conquering Saviour, is able to prevent every force that attempts to hinder the fulfilment of these plans.

Dearly beloved in the Lord, we must do our part in accomplishing God's plans for our life and God will always be faithful to do His part. The people around the world, who are becoming hopeless because of the sufferings and hardships they are passing through, will not hinder God or cause Him to fail to accomplish the good plans He has for them. He will bring them through their tribulations to live out the wonderful plans He has for them that will give them a future and a hope.

**You Are A Predestined Son Of God Ephesians 1:5**
**Chapter 6**

We commence Chapter 6 by turning to Ephesians 1:5 which says: "He predestined us to be adopted as His sons through Jesus Christ, in accordance with His pleasure and will."

As we have been developing Chapter Five, we discovered that God had a perfect plan for humanity - He prepared His two representatives so that through them He could accomplish His purpose of having children in His own likeness. But the first became disobedient to God, so God used immediately the second representative, Jesus Christ, Who was obedient to whatever God told Him to do before the foundation of the world. We are part of that input that God created in Christ before He made the world and we were predestined to be adopted children of God.

What we are now and what we are passing through can cause us to think that there are people who were predestined to be sons of God but also people who were predestined by God to be sons of Satan who perish with him. But, in the above chapter we have learned that God knows the plans He has for every human being. They are plans for good and not for disaster; they are plans to give a future and a hope to any human being who will allow God to adopt him or her as His son or daughter.

Because God had these plans for us, He predestined us to be His son or daughter through the fulfillment of those plans, giving us a future and a hope. Adam and Eve are grandparents, forefather and foremother of our parents. They produced our ancestors, our parents and us when we were already rebellious people to the will of God. And we became immediately children of the devil, who is the killer of the perfect plans made for us by God. The Jews told Jesus Christ that they were children of Abraham, but Jesus Christ told them that if they were children of Abraham they would behave like him. Christ proved to them that their father is the devil because their deeds were deeds of the devil, not of Abraham. Any descendant of Adam is a son of the devil, as it is proved by his/her deeds which are like the deeds of the devil. But mankind was not predestined to be sons of the devil, carrying out his evil plans. Satan wanted to win every human being for himself so he can use them to do his evil deeds. As soon as Adam, the first representative, gave him this opportunity, God used His second representative for humanity, Jesus Christ, Who will restore God's good plans for every human being so they can have the same plans God made for them: plans to give them a future and a hope. Once we have received Jesus Christ as Lord and Saviour, God adopts us as His son or daughter, and He begins to work these plans for our benefit, and to His glory as we become a part of the answer and not the problem: a support and solution to our needs and those of our family, our community, our nation and our world.

The antichrists always seek to reduce the divinity of Jesus Christ by discouraging those who are His followers, seemingly trashing their belief system and proclaiming that anyone can become successful in life without the help of Jesus Christ. But I want it known that no human being can accomplish anything without the help of Jesus Christ. The anti's may say that many have been successful without Him and that our secular nations prosper, despite the rejection of Christ. But I want all to know that everyone and everything is under the control of Jesus Christ, and if He wants, He can bring to nothing the results of whatever we are doing if we choose to continue rejecting Him. As people reject the Lord Jesus Christ, the King of kings and Lord of lords, they are rejecting the plans of their Creator for their lives. And, as they reject Jesus with their own plans, they are turning God's good plans for their lives to disaster. They are themselves turning God's blueprint for them to disaster: plans that could give them a future filled with hope. God has no favorites, but He delights to work with people who will rely on Him as they live here on earth, the earth made by God, Who is Almighty.

We are predestined to be a son or daughter of God. Have you, have I received Jesus Christ as Lord and Saviour so He can fulfil His plans for our lives? If not, we should do it now. The book of John 1:12-13 says that: "Yet to all who received Him, Jesus Christ, to those who believed in His name, He gave the right to become children of God - children born not of natural descent, nor human decision or a husband's will, but born of God." You and I are now a son or daughter of God by God's decision, and, in accordance with His pleasure and His will, once God adopts us as His child, He will no longer disown us. He made us His sons and daughters with all wisdom and understanding. But He expects us to be sons and daughters who will always do whatever He tells us to do so we can bring glory to Him as we praise Him through whatever we speak and through whatever we do.

**The Mysterious Plan Of God Revealed To You - Ephesians 1:9**
**Chapter 7**

Turn now to Ephesians 1:9 as we start the message of this chapter and see what God will tell us as we develop our subject. "God has now revealed to us the mysterious plan regarding Christ, a plan to fulfil His own good pleasure" (Life Application Study Bible).

**God has now revealed to us the mysterious plan regarding Christ.**

Maybe we can say that God has not yet revealed to us His mysterious plans regarding Christ. If we have followed carefully the above chapters, we will discover that we have already spoken about the revealed mysterious plan of God regarding Christ that is revealed to us. But let us develop this mysterious plan revealed to us by God.

This plan is to fulfil God's own pleasure. What do we think about God's pleasure, which He wants Jesus to fulfil? God's pleasure is to adopt us as His son or daughter so that we can praise Him and worship Him through Jesus Christ, our Saviour and Prince of Peace. We are in awe of what Jesus Christ is doing around the world through His servants. Jesus Christ is pursuing daily this plan as He fulfils it through His servants as they preach, teach and witness the message of the Word of Christ, which is continually restoring thousands of people around the nations of the world. As people are being restored by Christ through the message of the Word, Christ is reaching His goal of fulfilling the mysterious plan of God that is targeting all human beings so He can be praised and worshipped. There are people who have been passing through difficult situations but are now living in good conditions around the world. There are territories or countries of the world that were entangled in wars but are now peaceful. Undeveloped nations, towns and villages are becoming developed daily. People who were poor are becoming rich in families as they step into new opportunities. People who were in low positions are getting promotions. People who had no hope of being educated are getting degrees such as Doctors of Philosophy (Ph.Ds).People who had no possibilities of travelling are now moving around the nations of the world. People who had only one dollar in their bank account have now accounts with millions of dollars. People who had been sick are now healthy. People who were weak are now strong. People who were useless are now useful. People who had no hope have now a hopeful future. People who were a burden to others are now support to many people. The list of people who now live in good conditions after receiving the Word of God is endless. But whatever we have become (if we are not using charms) is the result of what Jesus Christ is doing as He fulfils the plan that is to fulfil God's own pleasure. I am not encouraging those who trust in charms for success, but let me discourage them, that as they use charms instead of trusting God, they are preparing disaster not only for themselves but for their descendants as well. People may say they are now living in good conditions because of their own potential and talent, or the potentials of their parents or politicians but we have to know that we are powerless without the help of our Lord Jesus Christ. Jesus Christ is the One Who empowers us in whatever we do. We can do everything through Jesus Christ, Who strengthens us. And without the help of Jesus we can do nothing (John 15:5).

We all come naked from our mother's womb and no-one can determine what we will become. If someone is born into a rich family, people conclude they will be rich like their parents. If someone is born into a royal family, people conclude they shall be king, queen, prince or princess, never lacking in anything. If someone is born into a family of people who have a high position in the government or international Non-Government Organization, people say that the child will have a high position like their parents. Children born into such families live with confidence, knowing that they will always be successful because they will inherit high positions from their parents. And children born into poor families often live with a mind-set that tells them they will follow in their parents' cycle of low positions and poverty. But I want to remind us all that, as Jesus Christ pursues the fulfilment of the plan that is to fulfil God's own pleasure, He can bring down those who are in high positions to low positions, especially those who are proud, and He can elevate the humble in low positions to a place of prominence. He can humble anyone who tries to hinder Him from fulfilling God's plan for someone else's life. And, regardless of their education or origin, He can promote anyone who is doing whatever He tells them, as they support Jesus in accomplishing God's plan. And, best of all, both those who are in high and low positions can be promoted to the very highest positions by God's grace, because God has no favorites.

**Everything was created through the Word.**

When we read the book of John 1 from verse 1 to 18, we learn about the wonderful work of the Word, Jesus Christ, Who was from the beginning. In the first verse we discover that in the beginning The Word already existed. This means that The Word, Jesus Christ, has no beginning, and when we continue reading the scriptures we discover that this Word has no end. This means that Jesus Christ is eternal. But you and I, we have a beginning and an end, whereas The Word existed from the beginning with God, and God created everything through Him; nothing was created except through Him.

**The Word gave life to everything that was created - John 1:4.**

Jesus Christ gave life to everything that was created and He still gives life to every creature that is created, including you and me. There is only one Creator, the God Who made heaven and the earth; He made everything that is visible and invisible through Jesus Christ. And Jesus Christ is the only One Who gives life to every creature, including every human being.

Although people are attributing the source of life to other origins, and various religions do their best to oppose Jesus Christ, there is only one truth. Don't be deceived by preachers and teachers who are down-looking Jesus Christ by attributing the source of life to other things. Jesus Christ has been given a name that is above all other names for time and eternity and no-one or anything can alter that eternal truth. This name has power to give life as God sees the necessity of the needs of any creature. Our life exists and is maintained by this One, Jesus Christ. When medical doctors are confronted with sicknesses and microbes in the human body, their desire is to eradicate and cure those illnesses, but they cannot do it without the help of Jesus Christ. So we should always use the name of Jesus Christ in our prayers because there are possibilities for every case as we use that name. And the result of using that name will give us the will of God for the case we are praying for. Jesus Christ is now seated at the right hand of God as He prays for you and me. Do we know that He is now presenting our needs to God on our behalf? He is continuously involved, praying for you and me. He knows God's plans for us for today, and He knows what we are passing through. He is presenting God's plans for our life to our Heavenly Father so that He can accomplish them, regardless of the sufferings, hardships and circumstances we are passing through. Therefore, we don't have to be discouraged but know that there is our High Priest, Jesus Christ, Who prays for us, and God hears and answers His prayers. The unchanging Jesus Christ, He is the same yesterday, today and forever.

**The Word made His home in us; He is full of unfailing love and faithfulness - John 1:14.**

Jesus made His home in us when we accepted Him as Lord and Saviour. We are His permanent home in which He is always working out God's plans for our life. When we become obedient to Him, we will stand in wonder as we see the results of our obedience. He is full of unfailing love, and this *Agape* love overwhelms Him to love people, unconditionally, without favouritism as He is faithful to accomplish God's plans for our lives. Some of God's people around the world have become well-known and popular because they have allowed Jesus Christ to make their bodies His permanent home, while others are popular because of God's grace. Remember that born-again Christians are God's vessels, and once Jesus Christ takes a permanent residence within them, He accomplishes God's purposes through them. And as they promote and exalt the name of Jesus Christ wherever they preach, teach or witness to the Word of God, He is giving them favour among the people. Throughout the Bible we discover that unknown people became known because they were preaching and teaching the Word they received from God. Maybe we can think that our being popular is not the result of our preaching and teaching of the Word of God or doing whatever God tells us to do, but I tell you that we are what we are by God's grace, and if we respond to the command of Jesus Christ, Who lives within us, we will receive more grace.

**Jesus Christ is the Way, and the Truth, and the Life - John 14:6.**

Jesus said: "I am the Way, and the Truth, and the Life: No-one comes to the Father except through Me."

**Jesus Christ is the Way.**

Jesus Christ is the only *Way* that every human being can pass through to reach God and obtain access to God's good plans for their life. The Bible tells us that this *Way* is narrow and only few find it. I believe that you and I are among those few who have decided to find it. This *Way* leads to life that is a new life brought about by Jesus Christ living within us. It means that this life of Jesus Christ flowing always through us can benefit other people as we empower them through encouraging words and actions.

There is another way called *wide*, and Jesus Christ said that many people pass through that *wide gate* that leads to destruction. Multitudes in the human race venture along that roadway because they choose to rely and depend solely upon their own strength or the strength of others to see them through life. But, without Jesus Christ, Who is the *Way*, they are under the leadership of Satan, enjoying the pleasures of sin for a season (Hebrews 11:25). Many people are choosing the *wide way* of immorality and wickedness, leading them to destruction without their recognizing it, while others have chosen this *wide way* of destruction, knowing they have purposely decided to enjoy worldly things for a season. They go about their own business excluding any association with God and Jesus Christ, Who is the *narrow way* that leads to life, and as a result they are reaping destruction in their lives.

**Jesus Christ is the Life.**

He is the *narrow Way* that leads to Life. He calls it a *narrow Way* because He incorporates His mysterious principles along the way as He pursues His plans of giving life to people. The way we do things is not the way God does things; God's ways are far superior to ours. Jesus Christ is the Good Shepherd Who gives His life for His sheep. The sheep, born-again Christians, listen to His voice. He calls His own sheep, born-again Christians, by name, and He leads them out to find green pastures. Jesus Christ, the Good Shepherd, knows us by name and, when He calls us He is expecting us to respond positively to His voice. He calls with the purpose of leading us where there are good green pastures: pastures where bornagain Christians can prosper as they eat fresh grass, the Word of God. When we hear Jesus
Christ calling us through His Word we have to respond positively because He is leading us to the fulfilment of God's plans for our life that we might currently be unaware of. But we will become aware of them as we reap the results of our obedience. He is calling us to give us life: a life that the world cannot offer.

Let us turn to the story of Naaman the Syrian in the book of 2 Kings Chapter Five. Naaman held the position of commander of the army for the king of Syria (Aram), and he was highly regarded in the sight of his master. It was through him that the LORD had given victory to Aram. Naaman was a valiant soldier, but he had leprosy.

One day, an Israeli girl who was serving in his household, told her mistress that if Naaman could go to the prophet Elisha in Israel, he could be healed of his leprosy. This word was conveyed to Naaman and when he arrived there, the prophet Elisha gave him instructions which he had to follow in order to be healed of his leprosy. But, when Naaman heard the instructions, "Go wash yourself seven times in the river Jordan then your flesh will be restored and you will be cleansed," he reacted negatively because Elisha himself had not approached him face to face, having instead sent his servant to the door with the instructions.

God's way of restoring Naaman's body was centred round the obedience of Commander Naaman to humble himself and wash in the Israeli river of Jordan rather than expecting to speak with the prophet face to face. But Naaman reacted badly after receiving the instructions from God through the prophet Elisha concerning his restoration. As soon as he heard the words of the prophet, Naaman went away angry, saying, "I thought that he, the prophet Elisha, would surely come out of his house to me, and stand, and call on the name of the LORD his God, wave his hand over the spot and cure me of my leprosy. Are not Abana and Pharpar, the rivers of Damascus, better than any of the waters of Israel?" So he turned and went off in a rage.

Many people react like Naaman as soon as they receive instructions from God through His Word concerning their problems. Naaman went away angry . . ."I thought that the prophet would surely come out to me . . ." His reaction could have hindered the restoration of his body because as soon as he heard the instructions, he went away angry, choosing to rely on his natural reasoning to receive his healing. The means he was thinking about could not help him because they were not from God.

In the New Testament Jesus Christ healed a leper but He did not tell him to go and wash in the Jordan River before He healed him. And there were many lepers in Israel and elsewhere who heard about Naaman's restoration, but they did not come to the Jordan River to wash themselves and be restored. Perhaps they knew that God does not use the same method every time to restore His people. We should always be obedient to any instruction given to us through His Word, and we have to know that, although many people may have the same problems, God is not bound to use the same method as He restores individually people's problems. When people become sick God can use different methods to heal them.

God uses mysterious means as He fulfils His plans, and He is the One to choose which means He uses as He accomplishes His purposes. We have to use always His instructions because, after using them, we will be filled with wonder when we see the results. And we will discover that they were mysterious means that God uses as He fulfils His purposes. We don't know better than God and our means are not God's means of accomplishing His will. So, we have always to do what He tells us to do by faith because the Bible says that the righteous, the born-again Christian will live by faith and not by sight.

Let us read Hebrews11:1: "Now faith is being sure of what we hope for and certain of what we do not see." This is the meaning of faith. As soon as we receive the instructions from God through His Word, we have to be sure of what we hope for, and we have to be certain of what we cannot see. It means that the Word we hear from God creates hope in our hearts, and we are certain that what we do not see, what we hope for, we will see happening as we expect and believe to see what God has promised in His Word. The book of Numbers 23:19 says:"God is not a man that He should lie: nor a son of man, that He should change His mind." Does He speak and then not act? Does He promise and not fulfil? No! God stands behind His Word to accomplish it, and every Word from His mouth cannot return to Him before It carries out God's will. So we should always obey God's Word.

Let us continue with the story of Naaman as we read 2 Kings 5:13-14: "Naaman's servants said to him, 'My father, if the prophet had told you to do some great thing, would you not have done it? How much more then, when he tells you, 'Wash yourself and be cleansed?' So Naaman went down and dipped himself in the Jordan seven times, as the man of God told him, and his flesh was restored and became clean like that of a young boy. 'My father', Naaman's servants told him, 'if the prophet had told you to do some great thing, would you not have done it?'" God asks us to do things that only a human being can do and we expect Him to do what only God can do when we obey His instructions through His Word. God cannot ask us to do what we are not able to do but He asks us to do what we can do. And after doing our part, we will see God doing His part that only He can do as He accomplishes His plans by His mysterious ways.

The example of Naaman teaches us that it is fruitless to try and adapt our own methods without searching for God's ways that bring solutions to our problems. We have to know that there was only one way for Naaman's restoration, and his flesh was restored and became clean like that of a young boy as soon as he applied the instructions from God through Elisha, the man of God. Even in our days, those who are applying the instructions from God through His Word, are being successful as they use God's mysterious means.

I remember someone telling me that "My life would not be successful in fulfilling the vision of God to plant churches around the world, ministering to hopeless people, because I have no financial backing." But, as he was trying to persuade me, I told him that, "We will fulfil it because we have God; therefore we are not relying on money for success but we are relying on God for success." And God is bringing new members to our church weekly, as well as opening opportunities leading us to success every week, despite the reality that we are experiencing severe hardships in Beni: like wars, rebels occupying our fields, killing people and kidnapping others.

Before we end this chapter, let us read now Mark 3:10: "For He had healed many, so that those with diseases were pushed forward to touch Him."

Jesus Christ used mysterious ways and means to accomplish God's plans and purposes for humanity. He healed many people, and when they heard all He was doing, they came from far and wide - Judea, Jerusalem, Idumea, Jordan, Tyre and Sidon - so that those with diseases pushed forward in the crowd to touch the LORD and be made whole. As soon as people heard about the healing ministry of Jesus, they immediately came to Him for help and, regardless of their conditions, they were all healed. And, whenever the people possessed by evil spirits saw Jesus, they fell down before Him, crying, "You are the Son of God."

As God uses us mightily to accomplish His plans, and as He brings to people the solution to their problems which were without solution, other people will hear about the wonderful things God is doing as He glorifies Jesus Christ. They will then come to Jesus Christ for help as God uses His mysterious ways to fulfil His plans and purposes.

Let us continue to search for the LORD and be committed to what He is telling us, because what He is telling us to do are mysterious means through which God fulfils His plans and purposes. And as we use these mysterious means through which God fulfils His plans and purposes, many people around us will come to Jesus Christ when they see the marvellous things God is doing through Christ and through us, the ambassadors of Jesus Christ here on earth. We have to know that it is God's pleasure to reveal to us His mysterious plans regarding Christ, and He reveals them through His Word.

**You Are Predestined According To The Plan Of God– Ephesians1:11**
**Chapter 8**

Turn now to Ephesians 1:11 ..."In Him we were also chosen, having been predestined, according to the plan of Him Who works out everything in conformity with the purpose of His will."

We are predestined, according to the plan of God given to Jesus Christ so that He can accomplish it. God has a plan for you and me that is according to the plan God made before the foundation of the world. And Jesus Christ has the mission of fulfilling it as He works out everything in conformity with the purpose of God's will. Jesus Christ knows God's plans for our life and He is able to accomplish them in conformity with the purpose of His will because He is Almighty.

All of mankind is included in God's plan, "For God so loved the world . . ." (John 3:16). God has a plan for everyone's life but not everyone seeks that plan for their life. Most of the world's citizens care nothing for their Creator, living as if He doesn't even exist. But God never disqualifies anyone, even when they are far from Him. He has a predestined plan, according to the will of God, and He forgets no-one. As was mentioned in a previous chapter, Saul of Tarsus never expected to come under the spotlight of Jesus Christ, but he wasn't forgotten; Jesus interrupted his evil plans in order to bring about His wonderful plans: that of turning him into a powerful weapon in the hands of God.

As Jesus Christ works out these plans in conformity with the purpose of His will, He opens opportunities to us, and most of the time these opportunities are given to us through the Word of God that always asks our obedience. And, if we don't obey what the Word is telling us, we may be missing opportunities that could lead to our predestined plan of God.

There is apathy among some Christians that it is acceptable to neglect prayer services because 'these services are for people who are not in a good financial situation or for people who have nothing else to do.' But we have to know that these services are for calling together both rich and poor, busy people and idle people, employed people and unemployed people. It is vital that all Christians, wherever possible, join together with other believers to meet corporately with the LORD of lords and King of kings to receive from Him that which no-one else can provide for us.

Let us learn from unnamed people in the Bible who were always meeting with Jesus Christ during their prayer services. Groups would gather together to pray, knowing and understanding that prayer is an absolute necessity as followers of Jesus Christ. Even Herod discovered as he did his research that the believers were performing miraculous signs and wonders because they had been with Jesus, both in prayer and in person.

As we meet always with Jesus Christ in church prayer services and in our personal secret place of prayer, through our meditating on the Word of God we often learn more from Him than that which any professor around the world could teach us. Do we know that Jesus Christ is the greatest teacher, Who uses His mysterious methods so that nothing can hinder Him from reaching His goal?

We may have learnt great agricultural techniques so we can always have an abundant harvest when we apply our learned skills. But, although we have learnt up-to-date agricultural techniques, we still can't prevent certain factors that can hinder us from producing a bountiful crop. We cannot control the weather and we cannot prevent circumstances such as our fields being occupied by rebels as in some areas of the Democratic Republic of Congo and other countries. But Jesus Christ cannot be overwhelmed by any factor or circumstance because He controls every factor, and even the weather is under His control. Because He is LORD, there is no circumstance that can stop Him from accomplishing what was predestined, according to God's plan. And remember that there will never be any power, authority or obstacle that will be able to stop Him from fulfilling His mission because He is the same yesterday, today, and forever (Hebrews 13:8). That means that He cannot change.

However, the one thing that does slow that plan down is our lack of faith and our disobedience. God cannot work in an atmosphere in which there is no faith. Disobedience and the lack of faith hindered God from permitting many of the children of Israel to enter the Promised Land of Canaan, a land flowing with milk and honey. Those who came from Egypt wandered in the desert for forty years until all the generation that had done evil in the sight of the Lord was consumed, except for Joshua and Caleb. When we read the books of Exodus, Numbers, Deuteronomy and Joshua, we learn much about the walk of the children of Israel with their God?

The book of Numbers 14:26-35 describes aptly the heart of God concerning His disobedient children; "The LORD said to Moses and Aaron, 'How long will this wicked community grumble against Me? I have heard the complaints of these grumbling Israelites. So tell them, 'As surely as I live, declares the LORD, I will do to you the very things I heard you say: In this desert your bodies will fall – every one of you twenty years old or more who was counted in the census and who has grumbled against Me. Not one of you will enter the land I swore with uplifted hand to make your home, except Caleb son of Jephunneh and Joshua son of Nun. As for your children that you said would be taken as plunder, I will bring them in to enjoy the land you have rejected. But you – your bodies will fall in this desert. Your children will be shepherds here for forty years, suffering for your unfaithfulness, until the last of your bodies lies in the desert. For forty years – one year for each of the forty days you explored the land – you will suffer for your sins and know what it is like to have Me against you. I, the LORD, have spoken, and I will surely do these things to this whole wicked community, which has banded together against Me. They will meet their end in this desert; here they will die.'"

And so it was that many of the people who came from Egypt died without entering God's plans for their lives because of their disobedience and lack of faith. God's plans for them were to enter and possess the Promised Land, the land of Canaan, which was flowing abundantly in milk and honey; such an abundant provision of foodstuffs. These plans were predestined according to God's plans, and God was working them out in conformity according to His blueprint made for them before the world began. But, these people complained at every obstacle they met along the way; every hardship became a point of contention. Finally they decided to put God and His chosen leader Moses aside, choosing instead to make their own god. They wanted to choose a leader who could lead them back to Egypt. And as the result of their disobedience, their lack of faith, and their rebellion against God, they all died in the desert without entering and possessing the land of Canaan, a land flowing with milk and honey.

The children of the Israelites, who survived the exodus from Egypt, were taught about obedience and having faith in God. And, as soon as they began to put their faith in God and obey Him, He permitted them immediately to enter and possess the land flowing with milk and honey - God's plans for their lives. No-one or any obstacle was able to hinder them from entering and possessing this land because they lived according to the principles set by God. Do we know that God's plans for our life are wonderful, like that of the Israelites? God's plans are like a land flowing with milk and honey, or like a land that is full of valuable minerals. To enter and possess our land, God's plans for our life, we have to increase our faith daily and be obedient to Him, regardless of the sometimes difficult circumstances we are passing through. Difficult circumstances are powerful elements that God uses to accomplish wonderful things: yes, miraculous intervention that only He can bring about, so let us learn about the power of faith.

We look at the story of Stephen. But, before we speak about Stephen, let us see first the source of faith. The Bible says in Romans 10:17: "Consequently, faith comes from hearing the message, and the message is heard through the Word of Christ"(NIV).

All the first believers of the first church were committed to participating in every prayer service so they could be taught the message of the Word of Christ by the apostles. They heard the message through the message of the apostles. Can you imagine the depth of God's knowledge that every church member had? Every church member was growing daily in the knowledge of God, and as a result, even Stephen, a deacon, was a man full of God's grace and power, doing great wonders and miraculous signs among the people. The Jews from Cyrene, Alexandria and the provinces of Asia became so obsessed to contend against Stephen's teachings that they began to argue with him, but they could not stand up to the wisdom or the Spirit by Whom he spoke (Acts6:8-10).

I believe that Stephen was full of God's grace as he was being equipped daily by the teachings of the apostles. And that grace produced power within him, which caused him to perform amazing miracles and signs among the people. Do we know that miracles or impossible things cannot be done without faith? And, "Faith comes from hearing the message, and the message is heard through the Word of Christ."

All the members of the first church had faith. And this faith, which was operating through Stephen as he preached the message of the Word of Christ, accomplished amazing results: "Many people from different areas could not stand up to the wisdom or the Spirit by Whom he spoke." His wisdom was born and growing in the Word as he was hearing and obeying the teaching of the apostles.

**The Word of Jesus is Spirit and Life.**
So Stephen grew in wisdom and the Word, which is Spirit and Life. He was familiar with the teachings of Jesus, Who, when facing opposition, reinforced the divine truth that *it was the Spirit giving Him wisdom that no-one could stand up against, regardless of their education or origin.*
Our churches are filled with people who are not committed in hearing the message of the Word which we teach, and as a result they have no wisdom or Spirit by Whom they can draw from as they contend with those who think they are wiser because of their education and origin. If every church member can acquire wisdom from the Word of God, people who think they are wiser may wonder as we share with them, because the wisdom we get from the Word of God is the highest wisdom, and its results always cause people to be amazed at its accuracy.
I regret so much when I see that most of our church members are not able to debate and stand up against the false teachings of Jehovah's Witnesses. I feel sadness when, in some churches only fifteen minutes is allocated to the preaching or the teaching of the Word. I wonder how members of such churches can grow in the knowledge of God and be able to exercise discernment when they come up against false teachings and false prophets, who are deceiving many people around the world as they steal their earthly goods from them. But if we, all church members of a local church, can be committed in continually hearing the message of the Word of Christ, we will soon win the world for Jesus as we share daily with people by the wisdom we have through this Word, His message. And our preaching and teaching in churches, on media, and by any other means we use for reaching people with the Gospel, because we will be possessing God's wisdom, which people cannot stand up against, our hearers will discover that God is the only source of wisdom. And they will come to Him for help.
Turn now to Hebrews11 as we develop the power of faith. In the first verse we discover that "Faith is being sure of what we hope for and certain of what we do not see."
**Faith is being sure of what we hope for.**
We are sure of whatever we hear from God through His Word and we hope for whatever God tells us. The Word says in Numbers 23:19, and it still applies today, "God is not a man, so He does not lie. He is not human, so He does not change His mind. Has He ever spoken and failed to act?"No. It is the reason why we have to be always sure of whatever God tells us. And we have also to hope for whatever He tells us, and if He tells us to do our part, we should be also committed to do our part in the proper time because He cannot fail to do His part.

**We are certain of what we do not see.**
Being certain is being convicted that God is able and He will do whatever He promised to do through His Word, regardless of the obstacles and circumstances. But we must believe that whatever God tells us that He will do, it will be done one day in God's timing, just as when He brought the visible world into being, as Hebrews11:3 tells us ... the universe was formed

at God's command, so that what is seen was not made out of what was visible.
If what is now visible was made out of what was invisible, why should we sometimes doubt what God tells us? He commanded, He spoke the Word, and the universe was formed. May we always remember that He still commands or speaks through His Word, and whatever He speaks is still happening in the visible world. Big ministries, churches and Christian organizations that are now impacting people around the world were founded on messages heard from within people's hearts, and as they believed that God was telling them through those messages to do something to expand His kingdom, God has caused the invisible vision to be seen through actions people are taking daily by faith. Ebenezer Evangelical Church International, the church in which I am Senior Pastor, is now growing weekly by faith, and God is providing for our daily needs because we are living by faith, not by sight. We are not living by what we see with our natural eye, like adverse circumstances for instance, but we are living by faith, trusting God to supply our needs, according to His riches in glory by Christ Jesus (Philippians 4:19).

The sixth verse of Hebrews11 says: "And without faith it is impossible to please God, because anyone who comes to Him must believe that He exists, and that He rewards those who earnestly seek Him." It is impossible for God to respond to people who live only by what they see with the natural eye. But God is pleased by people who live by whatever God tells them, although they have not yet seen it being done in the visible world.

We come to God through prayer because we believe that He exists, and as we come to Him we should be assured that He is pleased by our faith because we expect to have what we pray for without seeing any evidence of the answer for that which we are praying. And if He is pleased with our faith, He will reward us as we earnestly seek Him.

Verses 32 to 40 of Hebrews 11 speaks of people like Gideon, Barak, Samson, Jephthah, David, Samuel and all the prophets who lived by faith, achieving what anyone who is wise and faithful can achieve in God. Through faith they conquered kingdoms, they ruled with justice, they received what was promised, they shut the mouths of lions, they quenched the fury of the flames, they escaped the edge of the sword, their weakness was turned to strength, they became powerful in battle, they routed foreign armies, and women received back their dead raised to life again.

Because we are predestined according to the plan of God, Who works out everything for the fulfilment of His plan through Jesus Christ, so we should always receive faith from its source, the message of the Word of Christ. We should always live by faith because God is pleased by faith, rewarding those who earnestly seek Him by faith. He is not pleased however by people who live by sight, and He cannot reward them if they seek to reach Him without faith.

The reward that God gives to those who sincerely seek Him by faith is beyond the understanding of people around the world because the means God uses when He rewards those who are living by faith are special means that lead to victory and success.

**You Are Purposed for Praise of the Glory of Jesus Christ – Ephesians1:12**
**Chapter 9**
To begin Chapter 9 we will turn to Ephesians1:12: "In order that we, who were the first to hope in Christ, might be to the praise of His glory."
In this verse we have the personnel pronoun "we". The apostle Paul is speaking about we who first believed. He is speaking about the Jews, including himself, who believed in the Lord Jesus Christ. He is speaking about the members of the first Church, which was born after the Day of Pentecost.
**We, who first hope in Christ.**
The people of Israel and Judah were oppressed and aggressed by many nations and empires, like Babylon and Assyria, and Jesus Christ was born while these people were under the dominion and oppression of the Roman Empire. The people of Israel and Judah were expecting the arrival of the Messiah, Who is Almighty, and Who would be able to overthrow their oppressors and deliver them from the bondage they were in, as prophesied by the prophets.
As we develop the topic about the hope the Israelites had, let us read now Luke4:18-19: "The Spirit of the Lord is on Me, because He has anointed Me to preach Good News to the poor. He has sent Me to proclaim freedom for the prisoners and the recovery of sight for the blind, to release the oppressed, to proclaim the year of the Lord's favour."
Jesus Christ was born in Bethlehem and He grew up in the village called Nazareth, where He lived as seemingly being the son of Joseph, the carpenter. So people could not easily recognize Him as their Messiah, Who was sent by God, to deliver His people from their bondage. But in adulthood He was recognized by many of the ordinary people as the Messiah through the mighty deeds He was doing because the Spirit of God was on Him with the purpose of delivering God's people from their bondage.
His mighty deeds included:
- **Preaching the Good News through the power of the Holy Spirit**
- **Preaching and teaching with power and authority, causing miracles to happen.**

43

- **Healing every kind of sickness in Jesus' name.**
- **Raising the dead.**
- **Healing the deaf.**
- **Healing the dumb – those who were mute.**
- **Restoring sight to the blind.**
- **Healing the lame.**
- **Proclaiming freedom to the prisoners.**
- **Teaching the poor in spirit that they could become rich in spirit as they received the wisdom from on high.**
- **Delivering people from the dominion of Satan – people who were oppressed by demons.** Jesus Christ released the oppressed people who were dominated by Satan.

The worst oppression found in this world is satanic oppression because to be released from it requires supernatural power from God. Imagine if the head of a state is oppressed by Satan. All the peoples of that nation will suffer the consequences of his oppression. Imagine a family leader who is oppressed by Satan. What good can come from him for the benefit of his family members? Satan's oppression is leading to wrong decisions that cause leaders of nations, Christian organizations, families, etc., to oppress the people who are under their leadership. These deceived leaders are accomplishing Satan's mission of oppressing people so that those people cannot be successful in whatever they do. But we are no longer oppressed by Satan because Jesus Christ has freed us and we are indeed free. So we are for the praise of the glory of Jesus Christ, Who has released us from the oppression Satan put on us. We are now victorious and successful because Jesus Christ, Who has released us from the satanic oppression, is always on our side.

• **Proclaiming the year of the Lord's favour.** Everyone in Israel was eagerly waiting for the proclamation of this year of favour; a year of releasing the oppressed: a year of proclaiming freedom to prisoners: a year of recovering sight to the blind: and a year of preaching Good News to all of mankind.

Jesus Christ healed the sick; He delivered those who were possessed by demons; He recovered sight to the blind and He is still opening the spiritual eyes of many people today. He raised the dead; He cleansed lepers, and He performed many other miracles among the people to set them free. I believe these people, who were delivered by Jesus Christ, were no longer a burden or responsible for the problems being faced by their families and nations.

Whenever people begin to praise God and bring glory to Him because of what Jesus Christ is doing for them, unsaved people, who have influence on them, will always try to discourage them, even though, unbeknown to them, they too are purposed for the praise of the glory of Jesus Christ. People who are financially supporting families sometimes think they are the VIP in their families. But there are more Christian VIPs in our families and nations who are supporting us than what money and natural human ability is able to achieve. What money and human ability cannot do is achieve the results of the prayer of a righteous man. This prayer is powerful. It brings benefits to many people we are praying for, and yes, it brings wonderful results.

The followers of Jesus Christ had and still have the power and authority to do mighty miracles today. People who were then, and who are now, can be set free from Satan's prison-like grip because of the death of Jesus on the cross. When we enter into sweet fellowship with Christ He sets us free; we are no longer under Satan's dominion.

Our precious Lord performed so many wonderful miracles, causing the ordinary people to praise Him, and their praise brought glory to Father God. In verses 14 and 15 of this chapter we learn that news about Jesus Christ spread through the whole countryside and multitudes praised Him because of His powerful teaching and the mighty deeds He was performing among the people. The Jews saw many other miraculous acts that Jesus did among them, which have not been recorded in scripture. Sadly, many of the people who saw these mighty acts did not praise Him or bring glory to God. It is the reason why the apostle Paul said that "we, who first hope in Christ, might be for the praise of His glory." The Israelites first hoped in Christ the Messiah so they might be for the praise of His glory, but some of them did not bring Him glory because they did not praise Him.

Do you and I realise that both we, born-again Christians and the Israelites, were purposed by God for praise of the glory of Jesus Christ? God purposed all of us through Abraham, and we read this as we turn to Genesis 12:2-3: "I will make you, Abram, into a great nation and I will bless you; I will make your name great, you will be a blessing.I will bless those who bless you, and whoever curses you I will curse; and all the peoples of the earth will be blessed through you."

The nation of Israel was blessed through Abraham and his descendants – Isaac and Jacob, who trusted and hoped in God Almighty, and his descendants, who today, through the Messiah, live for the praise and glory of Jesus Christ. We who have received Jesus Christ as Lord and Saviour are blessed with our families and nations through Him, Who is a descendant of Abraham by His human genealogy.

Do we not see the wonderful things God is doing within our life since we became bornagain? There has taken place a great change in our life, and God is doing mighty wonders at our place of work, in our families, and in our nations. Some people think however that these positive changes are happening because of the potential of their politicians, managers, or the capacity of their family leaders. But men and women of God, some of whom we do not know, are praying daily for our work situations, nations, ministries, churches and families. And God is answering their powerful prayers, thus we see wonderful changes happening among the people around us, and we are hearing testimonies as many servants of God support ministries and churches in their daily prayers. Are we among those who are for the praise of the glory of Jesus Christ? Jesus Christ is performing His mighty deeds so that we may praise Him, and as we praise Him, we will be bringing glory and honour to Him.

So, dear brothers and sisters in the Lord Jesus Christ, we are purposed for the praise of the glory of Jesus Christ. We are what we are by God's grace, and we have what we possess by the ability Jesus is giving us because the Bible says that God is the One Who gives us the ability and the strength to prosper. Let us continue to praise Jesus for what we are and for the riches we have, and the glory will be to Him. And, once He becomes glorified through us in whatever we proclaim and through whatever we do, He will continue to increase our

45

wisdom, and He will continue to bless us in our country, and in whatever we do. All the praise and glory is for Jesus Christ, and every creature, including you and me, were purposed by God, before the foundation of the world, for the praise of the glory of Jesus Christ.

**You Were Included in Christ**
**Chapter 10**

Anyone, regardless of race, colour of skin, education or social class, is included in Christ when they hear the truth, the Gospel of Salvation being preached. But this hearing of the Gospel of Salvation that the apostle Paul was speaking about is not the hearing that takes no action to welcome Jesus Christ into our heart so we can receive Him as Lord and Saviour. Multitudes of people throughout the nations of the world have knowledge about Jesus Christ but instead of putting their knowledge into positive action, they turn it into a subject of negative debate, blasphemy, religious garbage or science fiction.

Praise God for people who preach and teach the truth, the Gospel of our Salvation. Praise God for the people who attend prayer services in which they are meditating on the Gospel of our Salvation and who know that they are already included in Christ. We were included in Christ as soon as we heard someone preaching the Gospel and welcomed Jesus into our heart to be Lord and Saviour of our life. And, if Jesus Christ is not yet abiding in your life, you can welcome Him into your heart through a short prayer and you will be included in Him. As soon as we are included in Jesus Christ, there is a supernatural life that begins within our lives: like hating the deeds of the flesh that were controlling us before we were included in Christ. Jesus Christ begins to live His life through us, which is a supernatural life. This is a supernatural life that enables us to live according to God's will among the unbelievers – the worldly people, the hypocrites and the antichrist - who generally speaking are always endeavouring to deter us from continuing to trust in Christ.

The Bible says: "I have been crucified with Christ; I no longer live but Christ lives within me" (Galatians 2:20). As soon as we hear the truth and welcome Christ into our hearts, He enters within us and removes the sinful deeds that were crucified with Him on the cross. And because we are now included in Him, we are not the ones who are living but Christ is the One Who lives within us. Therefore, for the rest of life we live here on earth, we live it for Jesus Christ, the Son of God, Who loved us and gave Himself for us, dying as our substitute on the cross like a criminal.

Many times we forget that we are included in Christ. Can people around us testify that we have been included in Christ when they hear what we say and see what we do? Is it really Christ Who is living within you . . . within me? There are those who are pretending to be included in Christ, and others who are included in Christ yet have become discouraged as they see the bad behaviour of those who are pretending to be included in Christ. We who are included in Christ must continue to live the rest of our life here on earth for Christ; we don't have to join those who have positions in churches yet are living their lives for themselves, defiling themselves as they speak and act like unbelievers.

May we remember that everyone individually will be accountable before God when Jesus Christ will come back to judge people according to what they did while they were still living. God will reveal even hidden secrets and there will not be any acceptable excuses. People grow disillusioned with churches because of the bad behaviour of some Christians,

but we have to know that another's bad behaviour cannot be an excuse before God that can hinder us from not living the rest of our life for Christ, Who loved us and gave Himself for us on the cross as our substitute. The Bible speaks also about being aware of the false prophets who are now among us and others who are yet to come. They put on sheep's clothing, the skin of a sheep, but inside they are predatory wolves. They pretend to be a humble servant of God, appearing to have a good motive for serving God's people, but they are robbers, killers and thieves, just like Satan their father, who is sending them. We need to be very vigilant and discerning, not allowing the wolves to get in and attack the sheep by robbing, stealing, and killing the faith of God's people. The finances and goods that rightfully belong to God's people are being stolen by wolves in sheep's clothing because of a lack of knowledge of the Word of God. Even business investments of God's people are sometimes ending up in the wrong hands as the Christian proprietors are deceived into believing God will prosper their misguided obedience. Marriages too, the union between a man and his wife which God has blessed, are also high on the list of the prowling deceivers, as they do the work of their father, the devil. I am not teaching against giving offerings so that people can be blessed by God; God bless those who offer according to the Scriptures.
We born-again Christians should always read, meditate on the Word of God, and give enough time for being taught the message of the Word of Christ so that we will no longer be infants, tossed back and forth by the waves, and blown here and there by every wind of teaching, and by the cunning and craftiness of men and women through their deceitful scheming (Ephesians 4:14). We will all grow and flourish in Christ in all things as we choose to be taught the message of the Word of Christ.
Once God exposes the deeds of the wolves, some followers of Christ become discouraged instead of thanking God for what He has done by exposing them. The exposure of the wolf has then exposed the vulnerability of the believer who has been caught up in the deception. If we have recognized wolves, the false prophets, we have to thank God because these deceivers can no longer hurt us because we have identified their deceitful techniques. We can then be a teacher to others who have not yet been deceived and hurt by these false believers. When I speak about false prophets I am speaking about any preacher or teacher of the Word of God who is not living what he or she is teaching but rather is living a life of pretence. I think that we have begun to identify those who are around us.
The Bible warns us that many false prophets will rise up and many people will follow them because of their deceptive miracles. I am not for one moment saying that anyone who performs miracles is a deceiver. The Bible clearly says in Mark16:17-18 that those who believe in Jesus Christ will perform also miracles in His name. I encourage those who know they are God's true prophets to live up to what they are teaching so there can be a distinction between God's prophets - those who live the Scriptures that they preach and teach- and false prophets, who, though preaching and teaching, don't live out what they preach and teach. As we are included in Christ, we have to ask God to give us wisdom and discernment so that we will not follow false prophets who are deceiving many people.
Sexual immorality is rife among false prophets, who blatantly say they have a covenant with

God that allows them to have sexual contact with church members. It is imperative they ask God for forgiveness for themselves and then for the church members they have duped into their deception. The Bible clearly warns that God will punish false prophets, and God will also judge those who are allowing themselves to be deceived by false prophets as they become their followers: a classic example of the blind leading the blind into a ditch (Matthew 15:13-14)! May we always remember that we are included in Christ and our spiritual leader has also to be included in Christ so he or she can lead us in the right way of going forward in God for His glory. Because we are included in Christ, we have to serve Jesus Christ without excuses because there is a reward and an inheritance for those who are included in Christ Jesus and live the rest of their life here on earth for Him, not for themselves.

Around the nations of the world many people have heard over and over again the Good News about Jesus Christ being preached through various means - the pulpit, the radio, the television, the telephone, and the Internet – or they have read the Good News through books, articles, tracts and E-mails. However, numerous people who are hearing the Gospel of their Salvation are not responding to it positively because of some excuses, of which God does not want to hear. God's purpose for any human being who hears the Word of God preached and taught through different means is calling whoever hears about it to welcome Jesus Christ into their heart so they too can be included in Jesus Christ, making Him Lord and Saviour. And as a result, they will get the benefit of being included in Christ, benefits that no human or worldly system can give.

**You Have a Deposit Guaranteeing Your Inheritance – Ephesians1:13-14**
**Chapter 11**

Turn now to Ephesians 1:13-14: "Having believed, you were marked in Him with a seal, the promised Holy Spirit, Who is a deposit guaranteeing your inheritance until the redemption to those who are God's possession - to the praise of His glory."

As soon as we believed in our Lord Jesus Christ and received Him as our Lord and Saviour, God marked us with a seal, the Holy Spirit. God placed a stamp within you and me, and this stamp is the Holy Spirit, and those who have this seal have become children of God. Our body is the temple of the Holy Spirit because He lives within us since the day we became a born-again Christian. This Holy Spirit is a heavenly deposit guaranteeing our inheritance. God has promised to give us an inheritance from Himself because we have believed in His Son Jesus Christ, after hearing about the work He did on the cross as our substitute.

Let us read Mathew 5:5: "Blessed are the meek, for they will inherit the earth." Meekness does not mean weakness but it means to be humble. People who have a deposit of the Holy Spirit, and people who are led by the Holy Spirit are expected to be completely humble as they wait to inherit the earth. What do we know about the earth we are expecting to inherit? God created this earth and He filled it with everything that will enable humanity, created in the image of God, to live here on earth without wanting for anything. But when Adam and Eve violated God's law, everything on this earth began to die because the Bible says that "the wages of sin is death" (Romans 6:23). Adam and everything on the earth were immediately cursed and God said that the heavens and the earth will pass away and He will create a new heaven and a new earth that will come down from heaven (see Isaiah 65:17 & Revelation 21:1).

May you allow me to describe it as we read Revelation21. We will describe this chapter verse by verse as we learn about our inheritance that the Holy Spirit is guaranteeing when He is deposited within us.

Verse1: "Then I saw a new heaven and a new earth, the first heaven and the first earth had passed away, and there was no longer any sea."

The apostle John received a revelation of a coming heaven and a new earth. God revealed what He is going to do in His timing. He will cause the first heaven and first earth to pass away, as He made them in the beginning (Genesis Chapter 1). And He will make a new heaven and a new earth. Those who have the Holy Spirit within them will inherit forever this new earth because they have a deposit guaranteeing their inheritance. Their inheritance is a new earth, which we cannot compare with this present earth, despite it being filled with riches, for many are the troubles of this world that rob mankind from enjoying the benefits of what they possess.

Verse2: "I saw the Holy City, the New Jerusalem, coming down from God, prepared as a bride beautifully dressed for her husband."

This inheritance, the new earth, is also called the Holy City. It is a city that will not be tainted with sinners or sin because every person who enters into this city will be holy, having conquered the power of sin through the indwelling presence of Jesus Christ. We will enter this Holy City after the resurrection and the transformation of our bodies when we meet Jesus Christ face to face. We will get new bodies, glorious and sinless bodies. Our inheritance is a Holy City, and the people of this city are holy people. We are the people of this city and we will live with our heavenly God and the holy angels.

This inheritance of ours is also called New Jerusalem. Jerusalem means *City of Peace*. There is a first Jerusalem; it was a Jebusite city in the hills of Judah. It was taken by David in the 10th century B.C to become the capital and holy city of the Israelites, the Jews (2Samuel5). Solomon made it a great city through his building program - temple, palace, and city walls. After the death of Solomon Israel was divided into two kingdoms:

1. The kingdom of Judah - its capital city was Jerusalem.
2. The kingdom of Israel - its capital city was Samaria.

In the period of the divided kingdoms Jerusalem was the capital city of Judah alone (1Kings14:21). In 586 B.C. it was destroyed by Nebuchadnezzar and many people died with the sword, others were taken to Babylon as captives, and a few were left in Jerusalem to live a life of misery (2Kings25). Then in 538 B.C. the process of rebuilding the temple and the walls made Jerusalem a great city again. The exiled came from Babylon after 70 years and they rebuilt the temple and the walls around Jerusalem, but again, in A.D.70, the city was destroyed; this time by the Romans (Luke 21:20), and since that time all those of Jewish descent have been scattered around many nations of the world.

But God is planning to make a New Jerusalem. This New Jerusalem will have an everlasting protection and there is no power that will be able to destroy it or scatter its people. The people of this city are those who have within them the Holy Spirit, Who is guaranteeing their inheritance, the New Jerusalem. This New Jerusalem will come down out of heaven from God. It will be prepared and adorned as a bride beautifully dressed for her husband. Just imagine how beautiful it will be. God is preparing this inheritance for us, and He has deposited the Holy Spirit within us to guarantee it for us until the redemption of we who are God's possession, to the praise of His glory. We are God's possession and He has prepared for us an inheritance that is guaranteed by the Holy Spirit within us. The Holy Spirit is guaranteeing our inheritance until the day Jesus Christ will come for the second time, and He will lead us into our eternal inheritance because we are God's possession. That redemption will glorify God and we will praise Him eternally for what He had being doing as He guarantees our inheritance forever.

Verse 3: "And I heard a voice from heaven saying, 'Now the dwelling of God is with men, and He will live with them. They will be His people, and God Himself will be with them, and be their God.'"

**Now the dwelling of God is with men and women.**

As soon as someone believes in the Lord Jesus Christ and receives Him as Lord and Saviour, God dwells within him or her, and God becomes Emmanuel - God with us. On that day it will be a visible dwelling of God for all those who received Jesus Christ as Lord and Saviour: those who have the Holy Spirit as a deposit, guaranteeing their inheritance of "God taking His visible dwelling with us" who are born-again Christians, walking according to His will.

**And God will live with us.**

He will live with us and we will see Him as He is. We presently see Him through His actions, and the conviction He is putting in us convicts us that He lives with us, but sometimes we forget that He is living with us because of the hardships we are passing through. But the day will come when there will no longer be hardships and limitations; we will see Him living always with us.

**We will be His people.**

We become God's people as soon as we receive Jesus Christ as Lord and Saviour, but on that day it will be a visible belonging to God. God Himself will be with us, and it will be seen that God is our God and we are His people.

**God will wipe every tear from our eyes.**

Verse 4 of Revelation Chapter21 says: "He will wipe every tear from their eyes. There will be no more death or mourning or crying or pain, for the old order of things has passed away." In today's society the world has become a dangerous place. People from different nations are passing through wars, hardships and sufferings, which are causing deaths daily, as in the East of the Democratic Republic of Congo. Rebels are taking cattle and other goods in Lubero territory, including Kitsombiro, my home village some years ago. Vehicles were burned along the way going to Goma from Butembo town, and many people were killed as they were going and coming from Goma, D.R.C. to Butembo, D.R.C. some years ago after 1994.There is endless mourning in Beni, D.R.C., and in other areas of Eastern D.R.C., as well as in other areas of other nations, including Somalia, South Sudan and Burundi. The total number of people who have been killed by rebels since 1994 in E.D.R.C. is now above the number of those who were killed in the genocide of Rwanda, with a tally of more than six million. And more than 350 people have been kidnapped by rebels in Beni town and Beni territory, as well as more than 400 people have been killed by those who might be ADF/NALU in Beni town and Beni territory since October 2014. The fields belonging to the people of Beni, which were filled with crops ready for harvest, are still occupied by rebels, so life has become problematic every day. There is mourning every day in Beni and North Kivu province as people lose their loved ones through evil killing sprees by different rebels. Although we are suffering pain and shedding tears every day: although we are mourning deaths every day, it is because we are still living in the old order of things. But when Jesus Christ returns we will live in our New Jerusalem with the new order of kingdom principles that will always be bringing to us endless happiness, for the glory of God. As we read in verse 4, we will discover that Jesus Christ will make everything new, and those things will endure forever. And these things are trustworthy and true, and they will happen in the New Jerusalem, our blessed inheritance.

**Jesus Christ is the Alpha and the Omega, the Beginning and the End.**

He is the only One Who is able to make every new thing that will endure forever and that will be for the benefit of mankind. Many businessmen and women, who do not have the fear of God, claim to make a new thing for the benefit of humanity, but most of these people are selling goods that are past their expiry date, thus causing many sicknesses and diseases within the bodies of people who purchased their products. But God will make a new thing for our benefit, and Jesus Christ will give us Living Water from the spring of Water of Life because we will be thirsty. This Water of Life is Jesus Christ Himself; He's the Word of God (John 1:1) and He gives liberally to those who are thirsty for Him.

**We who overcome will inherit all this.**

Revelation 21:7: "He who overcomes will inherit all this, and I will be his God and he will be My son."

The inheritance is for those who will overcome. Regardless of the circumstances, we have to overcome every temptation that we pass through, even if we pass through hardships that can test our level of commitment to doing whatever God tells us to do. We have to endure whatever we pass through for the glory of God. We must not give up in doing God's will. Christianity is for people who will overcome any situation, like their Lord Jesus Christ. Our Lord Jesus Christ overcame when He was here on earth pursuing His mission of saving humanity through His death on the cross as our substitute. He passed through many hardships, enduring them all, and God enabled Him to overcome and gain the victory every time.

As born-again Christians, our faith grows and matures as we endure hardships. The apostle Paul taught that we enter into the kingdom of God through hardships and tribulations, so we have to overcome these hardships and tribulations in Jesus' name. God is the One Who will enable us to overcome and inherit our inheritance, regardless of what we are passing through. But we have to know that God is on our side as we pass through problems, troublesome situations and/or difficult times. He will enable us to overcome if we will depend on Him. We born-again Christians are called to look heavenward, to lift up our eyes on Jesus Christ in every circumstance because without Him we can do nothing. He said: "When the Son of Man will come back, will He find faith on earth?" He already knew of the coming tribulations that born-again Christians are going to face as the world scene becomes increasingly more and more evil, "For" said He, "the love for God of many people will become cold" (Matthew 24:12). But, as we have learned, the inheritance is for those who will overcome.

If we want to claim our inheritance we must make that decision. If we want to be an overcomer we have to rely on the Lord Jesus Who enables us to do it. All our predecessors who had faith in God endured hardships yet they overcame. It is the reason why we are learning about the impact of their faith. May we remember also that today's great men and women of God are also passing through many hardships, but they are enduring, and as a result they are overcoming. They are becoming great men and women of God because they have overcome, but they will always need to continue trusting God daily to enable them to overcome hardships and tribulations so they can claim the inheritance God is preparing for them in His New Jerusalem. Never quit God's work because of hardships and tribulations but continue to endure because He is the keeper of our inheritance.

God will always be Almighty God to those who will overcome, and those who will overcome will be His sons and daughters. God's heart is not pleased with those who come to Him then, when they meet with hardships they give up, resorting instead to their own way, and, in the process become lost. He wants us to overcome any situation because God is always on our side through every hardship and tribulation, and, at the end He will still be our God and we will still be His children. Yes we are God's sons because we have believed in Jesus and received Him as Lord and Saviour. Let us determine to overcome any situation that seeks to hinder us from doing God's will so that we can be called sons of God who are able to overcome any obstacles, as He pursues His purposes in and through us.

In Revelation21:8 we see those who will not inherit the New Earth, and their place will be in the fiery lake of burning sulphur. These people are:

1. The cowardly
2. The unbelievers
3. The vile
4. The murderers
5. The sexually immoral
6. Those who practice magic arts

These people will die the second death: that is their being in the place in which there will be the fiery lake of burning sulphur.

In Revelation21:9-27 we see the inheritors of the New Earth and the description of our inheritance, the New Jerusalem:

1. The Bride, the Wife of the Lamb. There will be Jesus Christ and the Bride - the Church, all born-again Christians who overcome. These people are from all the nations of the world who will have their place in the New Jerusalem.
2. New Jerusalem is a High City, coming down out of heaven from God.
3. It will shine with the glory of God.
4. Its brilliance will be like that of a very precious jewel, like jasper, clear as crystal.
5. It will have a great, high wall with twelve gates and with twelve angels at the gates. On the gates there will be written the names of the twelve tribes of Israel.
6. There will be three gates on the East, three on the North, three on the South, and three on the West.
7. The wall of the City will have twelve foundations, and on them will be the names of the twelve apostles of the Lord Jesus Christ.
8. The walls and the gates of the City are measured by the angel with a rod of gold.
9. The foundations of the walls will be decorated with every kind of precious stone.
10. The walls will be made of jasper, and the City of pure gold, as pure as glass.
11. There will not be a temple in the City, because the Lord God Almighty and the Lamb is its temple.
12. The City does not need the sun or the moon to shine on it, for the glory of God gives it light, and the Lamb is its lamp.
13. The nations will walk by its light, and the kings of the earth will bring their splendour into it.
14. Its gates will never be shut, for there will be no night there.

15. The glory and the honour of the nations will be brought into it.
16. Nothing impure will ever enter it, nor will anyone who does what is shameful or deceitful, but only those whose names are written in the Lamb's Book of Life, God's Book of Life.
The Holy Spirit is within us to guarantee our inheritance, and once Jesus Christ comes back we will inherit this City, the New Jerusalem.

**You Are Remembered In our Prayers**
**Chapter 12**

Turn now to Ephesians 1:15-16:"For this reason, ever since I heard about your faith in the Lord Jesus and your love for all the saints, I have not stopped giving thanks for you, remembering you in my prayers."

All members of the Ephesian church were faithful in the Lord and they loved all the saints. The apostle Paul always gave thanks to God in his prayers for the quality and faithfulness of the saints in the church at Ephesus. To be faithful and to love all the saints is a good and well-pleasing sign that God delights in. Let us continue to be faithful to our Lord Jesus, and let us continue to love all the saints around the nations of the world, regardless of their denomination, race, education and/or social class.

I have discovered in many churches and Christian organizations that there are top leaders who are not committed in supporting successful members of their Christian organization in their daily prayers. My heart's cry to you is, "Don't abandon your people when they appear to be blessed by God in that which they've been called to. Stand with them in prayer. Mentor them as a father in the faith. Rejoice with them because of what God is doing through them. Encourage them as the Holy Spirit develops them in their ministries and gifts. And, be gracious and humble enough to open up opportunities that will enable them to grow spiritually in their calling."

It is of great concern when people give up serving in churches and Christian organisations because, instead of giving guidance and encouragement, their mentors put road blocks in their way, causing some to even give up trusting God for their growth and success. But we should know that even if our mentors, our spiritual fathers and mothers, retreat from supporting us in their giving of thanks and prayers, God has predestined many spiritual men and women who will always support us in their daily prayers as the Holy Spirit prompts them. This is now noticeably true in my life. But for over five years I was not aware of anyone supporting me in prayer. However, I thank God I now have one who is mentoring me, and many others lifting me up in prayer as the Holy Spirit reminds them. It is their prayers that will help enable us to reach the growth that God predestined for us, even as He sends His servants to mentor through messages from the Word of God. I want you to know that, although someone stops praying for you, there are many others who will faithfully continue praying for you. I am growing spiritually daily since I started sending my prayer support letters to best friends whom God has prepared to support me in their daily prayers, and I always see the profit and wonderful results of their prayers and powerful messages from the Word of God I am receiving from them.

The Bible says: "Ask and you will receive what you ask for" (Matthew 7:7). If we don't have friends who are supporting us sincerely with their prayer support, we can ask God to give us friends who will always give thanks to God for our spiritual growth and will always remember us in their daily prayer support. Knowing, or without knowing, there are people who are supporting us in their daily prayers, and we are seeing opportunities being opened to us because of the power of their prayers, bringing wonderful results for us in the kingdom of God.

Here are some encouraging verses from Ecclesiastes 4:9-12: "Two are better than one, because they have a good return for their work. If one falls down, his friend can help him up. But pity the man who falls and has no-one to help him up. Also, if two lie down together, they will keep warm. But how can one keep warm alone? Though one may be overpowered, two can defend themselves. A cord of three strands is not quickly broken."

If two people (or a group of people) are praying united and committed because they are better than one, they will have a good return for their praying. Let us continue to make known our prayer requests to men and women of God whom we trust so they too can support us in daily prayers as we pray also for their requests. We will rejoice together as we see the wonder-working power of prayer bringing amazing results. Their prayers will lift us up if we have fallen in our Christian life. Their continued prayer support will strengthen us if we have become weak. Even when we feel over-powered, with two or more petitioning the powers of heaven, we can win the spiritual battle, for, "You shall chase your enemies, and they shall fall before you by the sword. Five of you shall chase a hundred; a hundred shall put ten thousand to flight: and your enemies shall fall before you by the sword" (Leviticus 26:7-8). Praise God for the Sword of the Spirit (Ephesians 6:17)!

As we pray for one another, let us rely on God, because as we pray and believe, Jesus Christ is also praying faithfully for us whilst He is seated at the right hand of God. Are we looking for amazing results to our prayers, regardless of the situations we are in? Remember that God never gives up His plan. It is the reason why He cannot stop connecting us with new men and women of God who support us in their daily prayers so that He can fulfil His wonderful plans concerning us. Most successful well-known Christians are prayerful people, having other prayerful men and women of God who also support them in prayer. Even other people around the world who do not know God can also become great because of the prayer support of their family members who are committed to praying for their success. Men and women of God who are committed pray-ers are called spiritual warriors because they lift up and support others in their daily prayers. It means that we are supported in prayer by spiritual warriors known and sent by God for this purpose. And, as soon as they start praying, they begin to witness wonderful results because God has sent them for this reason.

There are some people who are deceitfully requesting money from other believers when they pray for them; money for food and/or transport etc., stating that it is God's answer to their prayers. But did they actually pray or fast for God's provision by faith or by greed? Then they use any acquired money for their own purposes. These are deceivers and God cannot even hear them if they pray.

But people who are supporting God's people in their daily prayers are not asking for any financial gain for their prayers because they are sent by God, Who will reward them for the work they are doing. And, men and women of God who are mentoring God's future servants through messages from the Word of God are not asking payment for what they are doing because they know that they have been sent by God and God will reward them for the work they are doing.

Men and women of God from around the world are remembering our nations in their daily prayers as they pray for peace to return in South Sudan, Burundi, Somalia, Democratic Republic of Congo and other nations that are in wars, and we are seeing God moving as they pray and believe that we will soon reap the amazing results of their prayers.

The power of prayer is invisible to our natural eyes but we see it by its results, although some people can attribute the results of prayer to their ability or to other forces. Those who live by faith are prayerful people, and the result of their faith and the prayers of others who are supporting them have always been wonderful and will continue to be wonderful because the prayer of a righteous man or woman will never lose its amazing power. If men and women of God were to tell you how God is enabling them to do whatever they are doing by faith, they would tell you that they are praying, and God is causing invisible things to become visible: therefore, never under-estimate the power of prayer and the faith of those who pray them.

**You Are Purposed by God to Be Given a Spirit of Wisdom and Revelation – Ephesians1:17**
**Chapter 13**
**"I keep asking that the God of our Lord Jesus Christ, the glorious Father, may give you the**
**Spirit of wisdom and revelation, so that you may know Him better."**
The apostle Paul kept asking God to give the members of the Ephesus church a spirit of wisdom and revelation, so that they may know God better.
Let us develop this chapter as we insert three elements found in the writing of Calvary Community Church about discipleship. I will only list three elements from the topic *"Understanding God"* and I will develop them as God will reveal insight to me in the verses quoted so that we can understand this chapter that I am now developing.
In the first point of the topic *"Understanding God",* there is written the follow sentences:
How Can I Know God?
I can know God because He has revealed Himself. The revelation of God is not restricted to the Bible. There are many ways in which God has shown Himself to man; we will consider three.
A. GOD HAS REVEALED HIMSELF IN CREATION -- Romans 1:20
B. GOD HAS REVEALED HIMSELF IN THE BIBLE -- Hebrews 1:1
C. THE COMPLETE REVELATION OF GOD IS FOUND IN JESUS CHRIST – Hebrews 1:2-3; Colossians 2:9
The above three ways were written by Calvary Community Church. Now may you allow me to develop these three ways in which God has shown Himself to man so that He can be known better. I will use other words as God reveals them to me. The verse we first quoted in Ephesians1:17says that God has to give us wisdom and revelation so that we may know Him better.

**God has revealed Himself in creation – Romans1:20**

"For ever since the world was created, people have seen the earth and sky. Through everything God made, they clearly see His invisible qualities- His eternal power and divine nature. So they have no excuse for not knowing God."
The apostle Paul prayed continually for the Ephesus church so that every church member would know God better. As we read the above verse, we discover that God has made Himself known to everyone, having given them the five senses, or at least some of them, as we see the world that God created. Let us list first the five senses:
1. To hear: Everyone is hearing that God is the Creator of both the visible and invisible so that He can be known better by everyone.
2. To smell: By the sense of smell people can identify what is happening around them. God has made us able to distinguish between a pleasant and an unpleasant smell. Through this sense we can identify the beautiful perfume of a rose to the nauseating

stench of a dead animal. It is God alone Who has created us with such capacities.
3. To touch: As we touch something, we will immediately have information about it, even if we are in the darkest place – is it hard or is it soft? Is it wet or is it dry? God has created us with this ability so that we can know Him better through His creation.
4. To taste: When we taste something we are able to distinguish between many kinds of foods. Our taste buds are individual to every one of us, which is why we all differ in our likes and dislikes of food. God has a purpose of making Himself known to us through taste; that is the reason why He created us this way.
5. To see: The gift of sight is a wonderful, precious miracle that enables us to see the diversity of all nature and the creatures God has made. We discover that through sight God is revealing Himself to us for the purpose of making Himself known to us.

God created everything and everyone with a purpose; He did this through His mighty, invisible, divine power so that we can have wisdom and revelation that will enable us to know Him better. James1:5 encourages us that "If any of you lacks wisdom, he should ask God, Who gives generously to all without finding fault, and it will be given to him." We need a heavenly wisdom so that we can know God better, so let us ask in prayer and it will be given to us.

Mankind stands before their Creator, having no acceptable excuse to deny the existence of their Creator. All nature verifies that there is a higher power Who has manifested Himself through His handiwork to the world. We must never allow Satan to blind our eyes or our minds to the fact that God is the Creator of all things – not evolution and its evil teachings.

## God Has Revealed Himself in the Bible – Hebrews 1:1

Here is what is written in Hebrews 1:1: "In the past God spoke to our forefathers through the prophets at many times and in various ways." The writing of the prophets represents God speaking, as recorded in the Bible. All the writings of those who contributed to the writing of the Bible were also inspired like the prophets. Once we have asked God to give us wisdom we can know Him better because we have also the Spirit of revelation within us, revealing God to us in a deeper way as we read the Holy Scriptures.

The book of John1:1 says that: "In the beginning was the Word, and the Word was with God, and the Word was God."The Bible is called the Word of God and this Word is God Himself. When we ask God to give us the Spirit of wisdom and revelation we can know Him better, as the Spirit of wisdom and revelation within us leads us to a better knowledge of God as we read the Scriptures found in the Bible. God is hidden in the Scriptures, the Bible, but we need first the Spirit of wisdom and revelation so that God, Who is hidden in the Scriptures, can be revealed to us through His Word, with a purpose of knowing Him better.

## The Complete Revelation of God is Found in Jesus Christ – Hebrews 1:2-3; Colossians 2:9

Turn now to Hebrews 1:2-3: "But in these last days He (God) has spoken to us through His Son, Whom He appointed heir of all things, and through Whom He made the universe. The Son is the radiance of God's glory and the exact representation of His being, sustaining all things by His powerful Word. After He had provided purification for sins, He sat at the right hand of the Majesty in heaven."

In this chapter we are developing a topic that says, "You have been purposed by God to be given the Spirit of wisdom and revelation." Jesus Christ, Who is now living within all bornagain Christians, is the exact representation of the being of God. So we should always ask

Jesus Christ to give us the Spirit of wisdom and revelation so that we can know God better. Jesus Christ, Who is not only the exact representation of the being of God but He sustains also all created things by His powerful Word. He (Jesus) is now seated at the right hand of the Majesty in heaven as He prays for all born-again Christians, that we may grow and mature towards a better knowledge of God. And we cannot know God better if we don't have the Spirit of wisdom and revelation.

So we need wisdom and revelation from God so that we will be able to know God better. And we get an increased wisdom and revelation from God as we search for it, as we pray daily, read the Bible daily, and meditate on its Word. Do we understand why many people neglect God's business of preaching and teaching the Gospel? The answer is this. They don't have wisdom and revelation, which can lead them to know God better. People have misunderstood God because of their lack of wisdom and revelation that could lead them to know God better.

In East Africa and other parts of the world, many people are committed in serving God and in giving of their finances for supporting God's business of preaching and teaching the Gospel. However, it is the opposite in many areas of the Democratic Republic of Congo and some other nations, where only few are committed in serving the Lord, only few support God's business with their finance, and only few parents encourage their children to become fulltime ministers of God.

I believe the reason why people can be committed as they serve God and abundantly support finances to God's business of preaching and teaching the Gospel is because they are getting an increased wisdom and revelation that leads them to know God better. This daily increased wisdom and revelation is encouraging them to consider God's business as the highest priority which needs our time, money and commitment.

**The Eyes of Your Heart are Purposed to Be Enlightened–Ephesians1:18**
**Chapter 14**

Turn now to Ephesians 1:18 as we begin developing Chapter 14: "I pray also that the eyes of your heart may be enlightened in order that you may know the hope for which He has called you, the riches of His glorious inheritance in the saints."
The apostle Paul received an encouraging report from the church of Ephesus. The members of the church were faithful and had unfailing love for all the saints. But Paul continued to pray for them so that the eyes of their heart may be enlightened.

**The eyes of your heart may be enlightened.**

The human body has two kinds of eyes: the physical eyes and the eyes of the heart, called also spiritual eyes. We use our physical eyes to see created visible things around us, such as mountains, lakes and people, and we use the eyes of the heart, spiritual eyes, as we search for God's hidden secrets within His heart, within us, within creation, within the Bible, within the Holy Spirit, within Jesus Christ.
Paul teaches us that these eyes have to be enlightened, and our scripture verse says that Paul was praying for the Ephesus church members so their eyes may be enlightened. So, praying daily for the eyes of our heart to be enlightened will permit God to enlighten our spiritual eyes, the eyes of our heart. If it was necessary for Paul to pray this prayer, it reinforces the Biblical fact that we too have eyes of the heart that have to be enlightened by God as we and others support us in their daily prayers.
Once God has enlightened the eyes of our heart we should be able to know the hope to which God has called us. God has called for us from darkness to light with a purpose of giving us hope. There is hope for us who have been called by God to be His servants, and this hope comes through having the eyes of our heart enlightened. Without spiritual eyesight it is difficult to maintain hope; it is difficult to serve our Lord Jesus Christ in a positive manner. Without the eyes of our heart being enlightened we will speak negative words; we will not perceive the hidden things of God that give us hope.

**The riches of God's glorious inheritance in the saints.**

There are riches of God's glorious inheritance within every born-again Christian. But these glorious riches are hidden to many people because the eyes of their heart have not yet been enlightened by God, or they are not willing to ask God to enlighten their spiritual eyes, the eyes of their heart. These glorious riches are within us if we have received Jesus Christ as Lord and Saviour. These are spiritual, glorious, hidden riches that can be seen if our spiritual eyes are enlightened. And once we have seen these glorious riches within our heart it will motivate us to greater heights in God as we see the possibilities He purposed within us before the foundation of the world. Do you know that Jesus Christ is these 'glorious riches of God' which are within us? And once we discover that Jesus Christ is the 'glorious riches' we have, we will begin living as sons and daughters of the Most High God, seeing ourselves of great value in God's eyes because we are containers of Jesus Christ, Who is precious and above all earthly riches.

Generally speaking, the world's standard of measuring is money . . . "If you have money, you have life!" But we born-again Christians say: "If you have Jesus, you have life!" Let us say it this way: "If you have Jesus Christ, you have life, you have riches within you, and you have riches with you."

People may say that "these are only spiritual riches that will not cause one to have earthly riches." But they should know that God is the One Who gives people the ability to be a financial success because without Him we can do nothing. If the eyes of our heart are not enlightened we may always live in deception, attributing the source of the possibilities and riches within us or within other people to ourselves or to other sources.

God is Spirit and He wants to reveal to us His hidden secrets through the eyes of our heart. But these eyes have to be enlightened first. And God is the only One Who can enlighten them.

My prayer is that God may enlighten the eyes of yours and my heart, in order that we may know the hope to which He has called us. May He enlighten us to recognize the riches of God's glorious inheritance that lies within us. People love God more because of the knowledge of God they have acquired. People's hope rises as they see through the eyes of their heart: as they see through their spiritual eyes direct revelation from God, fulfilling His promises.

**The Incomparably Great Power for Us Who Believe in God–Ephesians1:19-20**
**Chapter 15**

Let us read Ephesians1:19-20: ". . . And His incomparably great power for us who believe. That power is like the working of His mighty strength, which He exerted in Christ when He raised Him from the dead and seated Him at His right hand in the heavenly realms."
The apostle Paul prayed for the Ephesus church members so that they could know also the incomparably great power for us who believe. We who believe in the Lord Jesus Christ, we have great power within us that we cannot compare with other great powers known around the world. The great power we have within us is the working of God's mighty strength. It means that God's mighty strength is for you and me; it is within us. The above verses are saying that this incomparably great power God exerted in Christ when He raised Him from the dead is the same incomparably great power that God has inserted within us when we received Jesus Christ as Lord and Saviour. This incomparably great power, which is now for us who believe, is the same incomparably great power that seated Jesus Christ at the right hand of God in the heavenly realms.
If this incomparably great power raised Jesus Christ from the dead and it seated Him at the right hand of God in the heavenly realms, that same power can do whatever God wants to do through us. But God cannot use mightily this incomparably great power within us if we have not yet known it is within us, and if we have not yet known that it is for us who believe. If we continue to pray as we meet with other believers during Christian meetings, we will know this incomparably great power for us who believe. And once we have known it we will know God better as we see Him using mightily this power He has inserted within us as He accomplishes His purposes. And this will encourage us to be committed to serve our God as we see the results of what He is doing through us, as we impact people around the nations of the world through His incomparably great power that raised Jesus Christ from the dead and seated Him at the right hand of God in the heavenly realms.
If this incomparably great power raised Jesus Christ from the dead and seated Him at the right hand of God in the heavenly realms, it is the only great power that can solve any human problem, beginning first with sin, which is the highest cause of problems found in this world.
We preachers and teachers of the message of the Word of Christ bring the Good News that can transform someone's life through the incomparably great power found in the Word of God. This is an invisible incomparably great power that sometimes we don't see the immediate results of with our physical eyes. But we may see the result of what this power is doing after some days, months, or years, and if God chooses we can see the results of it as soon as we use it, as we preach or teach the powerful Word of God which contains this incomparably great power that raised Jesus Christ from the dead, seating Him at the right hand of God in the heavenly realms, far above any evil spiritual force.
The incomparably great power within you and me may impact thousands of people around

the world of whom we have no knowledge. As we move in this power, God can respond to our faith and touch anyone, anywhere in the world, and we will not be aware of the wonderful results until we reach heaven. Then we will be full of wonder when the Lord affirms to us how this incomparably great power that was operating within us has impacted people around the world. And, if it happens even when we are still here on earth that God expresses this to us, we will be even more committed to serving Him than we are.
This great power working within us is like the natural power of a seed that we plant in the soil. We plant a seed and the natural power or strength that is within it causes it to spring forth with new life. But if it is a dead seed it will never geminate, grow and produce fruit. Likewise, when we use the power or strength that is God-given within us, it will bring forth and reproduce to fulfil its purpose. The incomparably great power that is for us and that works within us is able to give spiritual life even to a dead seed: someone who is spiritually dead. And this same power that has given life to someone who was spiritually dead will also be able to make them grow spiritually and become mature in the knowledge of God.
Turn now to Isaiah45:22: "Turn to Me and be saved, all you ends of the earth; for I am God, and there is no other." There is a mighty great power that is able to save every person condemned to die, every ruined person and every lost sinner. The incomparably great working power is able to save every person who was born in sin, and who have lived in sin; this power is able to redeem even the chiefest of sinners.

**What this incomparably great wonder-working power of God can do.**

This incomparably great wonder-working power is an all-sufficient power, able to save any and all hopeless sinful people in the nations of the world if they turn to the God of Abraham, Isaac and Jacob to be saved, for He is the only God - there is no other. Jesus Christ is the only One Who is able and willing to save the very chiefest of sinners. He finished His redemption work on the cross, after dying like a criminal, thus enabling Him to love and die for the ungodly.
This mighty great wonder-working power enabled God to create everything, visible and invisible. And when mankind broke God's law, it enabled Jesus Christ to appear in the world as *'God manifest in the flesh'* to redeem man and woman, created in the image of God, from the curse of the law, being made a curse for us. This incomparably great power enabled Jesus to give Himself for our sin, and He died on the cross as our substitute. This same power enabled Jesus Christ to forgive all our sins, and His Word says that if He has forgiven us He will never remember our sins because His mighty power is able to forgive every sin and forget it forever (Psalm 103:12). This power enables God to be faithful and to accomplish all His promises in His time as He purposed them before the foundation of the world. And it enables Him to work out every detail of His plans in conformity with the purposes of God Who made them, accomplishing them in the proper time He fixed for every activity under the sun.

This incomparably wonder-working great power also:

• Enables God to adopt a lost sinner as His son or daughter.
• Enables God to make him/her a saint.
• Enables God to blot out the sinner's name in the book of death and write their name in the Book of Life.
• Enables God to call the adopted one His son or His daughter.
• Enables God to make the adopted ones His chosen people –
1 Peter 2:9-21.

Those listed below are found in these verses.

• Enables God to make those who were disobedient a royal priesthood.
• Enables God to call His people holy - those who were born in sin and lived in sin.
• Enables God to make us a holy nation.
• Enables God to make us a people belonging to Him.
• Enables us to declare the praises of God Who called us out of darkness into His wonderful light.
• Enables God to make us the people of God: we who were not a people.
• Enables God to be merciful to us: we who had not received mercy.
• Enables us to live as visitors and strangers in the world.
• Enables us to abstain from the sinful desires that war against our souls.
• Enables us to live a holy life among ungodly, that, though they accuse us of doing wrong, they may see our good deeds and glorify God.
• Enables us to submit ourselves for the Lord's sake to every institute of authority among men: be they kings, as the supreme authority, or governors, who are sent by God to punish those who do wrong and to commend those who do right.
• Enables us to do good as we silence the ignorant talk of foolish men.
• Enables us to live as free men and women because we do not use this freedom as a cover-up for evil.
• Enables us to live as servants of God.
• Enables us to show proper respect to everyone.
• Enables us to love one another.
• Enables us to fear God, to hate sin.
• Enables us to honour the king, the rulers.
• Enables us to be submitted to our masters with all respect, not only to those who are good and considerate, but also to those who are harsh.
• Enables us to suffer for doing good: to endure this suffering because it is commendable before God.
• Enables us to follow in the steps that Jesus Christ left us as an example of enduring suffering for God's sake.

God's incomparably great wonder-working power can do what we cannot do and what we cannot imagine. It can do what is beyond our understanding. It can cause to happen whatever God wants to perform without anyone's help, and it works without the intervention of any outside influence; no force can hinder Him from accomplishing what He has in mind, as He moves in His incomparably great power for us who believe.

His power is also able to change and transform any circumstance around us. It is able to move mountains or problems as it turns impossible situations into victories. No obstacle is able to stop the hand of God from accomplishing His will.

This power is able to make rivers in the desert. It is able to make ways to success where previously there were obstacles and closed doors preventing the people of God from moving forward. It is able to change a beggar into someone who can be a support to thousands of people. It is able to promote the poor from the dust, a lowly position, to be seated in high places of honour. It is able to heal every sickness and it is also able to heal and restore any broken heart, despite its degree of brokenness.

In short, this incomparably great power for us who believe is able to accomplish God's will in His time, regardless of the circumstances. So, let us continue to pray that this incomparably great power can be known by we who believe in the Lord Jesus, and let us be continuously available so that this incomparably great wonder-working power can always accomplish God's perfect will and plans through us, as we impact people around the nations of the world.

**Jesus Christ Is Seated Far Above All Powerful Forces – Ephesians1:20-21**
**Chapter 16**

Turn again to Ephesians 1:20-21 as we commence Chapter16. "And His incomparably great power for us who believe: that power is like the working of His mighty strength, which He exerted in Christ when He raised Him from the dead and seated Him at His right hand in the heavenly realms, far above all rule and authority, power and dominion, and every title that can be given, not only in the present age but also in the one to come."
These verses say that Jesus Christ is seated at the right hand of God in the heavenly realms, far above all rule and authority, power and dominion, and every title that can be given, not only in the present age but also in the one to come. He, the Lord Jesus, is seated at the right hand of God and He is interceding for us – Romans8:34. Let us now develop this chapter as we insert in it the words found in the above verse.

**Jesus Christ is seated far above all rule and authority.**

When we read the book of Ephesians 6:10-19, we discover there are evil rulers and evil authorities in the heavenly realms. These rulers and authorities are evil spirits that are under the command of Satan. Their purpose is to control the peoples of the earth through demonic actions so that Satan's plans and purposes can be carried out and fulfilled on earth: the plans and purposes that lead men and women to live wickedly as they rebel against God, their Creator.
But our verse says that Jesus Christ is seated far above all these rulers and authorities and He is interceding for us so that we can continue to live according to God's plans and purposes during our time here on earth.

**Jesus Christ is seated far above all power and dominion.**

There are in the heavenly realms evil spirits that have powers and dominions. These evil powers and evil dominions are there for the service of Satan, using their powers and dominions to influence people to live selfish, sinful lives that fall into Satan's evil trap.
But our Lord Jesus Christ is seated at the right hand of God, far above all evil powers, all evil spiritual forces, and all evil dominions. And He is interceding for us day and night so that we
66
can continue bringing glory to God as we accomplish His will and plans on earth to expand His Kingdom.

**Jesus Christ is seated at the right hand of God in the heavenly realms, far above every title that can be given in the present age, the present world.**

There are titles given to men and women throughout the world who are employed in different spheres of engagement, like president, minister, governor, mayor, general major, commando, honourable gentleman, etc. There are also other titles given to people in churches and Christian organizations - titles like Pope, Cardinal, Archbishop, Bishop, Apostle, Prophet, Pastor, etc. There are also other titles that are given to men and women like professors, doctors, scientists, billionaires, and every other title known in this present age. There is a hidden power and authority within every title which is given to men and women in this present world. Titles can also be called powers and authorities because people who have been given titles always use these titles, powers and authorities so that they can accomplish their task. They command people to accomplish their will, but if they are not under the influence of the Holy Spirit they may oppose that which is good, not knowing God's will or plans for people's lives, families, churches, Christian organizations, nations, etc.

Praise God that our Lord Jesus Christ is seated at the right hand of God in the heavenly realms, far above all titles that can be given to men and women. And He is supporting us in His daily prayers so that God's plans for our lives may be fulfilled, regardless of the powers and authorities which are trying to reduce God's plans for our lives to nothing. Even in some families there are people in their clans who have high titles, which they use as an authority to dictate final words and final decisions for the members of their families. The only One Who has the final Word or final decision for someone's life is God because God's Word or God's decision for someone's life will always bring wonderful results for our good and for the good of the people around us.

Dear brothers and sisters, we should always seek God as we use titles, powers and authorities given to us by God or by God through other people, so that our decision can meet God's plans or decisions for the betterment of other people. If our decisions meet God's decisions, we will be part of other people's successes and victories as they live and carry out their daily responsibilities and businesses.

May we always remember the Bible says that "all authority is from God." We have been given our title, powers and authorities by God through people. For God is the One Who purposed our inner potentials before the foundation of the world, and it is He Who opens opportunities to receive titles for His glory, as we use our given powers and authorities to strengthen and encourage those under our authority.

The father of Antipas Mbusa Nyamwisi, a popular member of the opposition party in the Democratic Republic of Congo, died this year, 2015, in Beni, and the governor, Julien Paluku Kahongya of North Kivu province, D.R.C. attended the funeral service at which he was asked by journalists to speak about the life of the one who had passed away. His words spoke of a humble and simple man who had a listening ear for any and all who approached him, therefore encouraging the listeners to also adopt these special qualities– humility, simplicity and an attentive ear.

Many people who were once popular in their society have lost their positions because they were not humble and simple, nor did they have ears that were open to the concerns and cries of the people. They ignored and neglected people in low positions, respecting only those who held high positions like themselves. This grouping of people support only those to whom they think they can benefit from, thus, the very people in low positions who can be a support for their destiny are held in very low esteem.

People who use their positions to oppress and dominate other people have no knowledge that God is the One Who gives high and low positions among mankind. God is able to humble someone who is in a high position and give the highest position to one who had 'come from the bottom level'. Everyone, regardless of their high or low position, has to continue to be humble and simple, with a listening ear that builds up one another for the glory of God. As we use our title for God's instrument of strengthening and encouraging people, God opens higher positions for us because the Bible encourages us that "someone who is faithful in little things will be put in charge of many things" (Luke 19:17).

A high position is not what most people think about, but maybe we are among those who are considering a high position in this world. These positions will be given to those God predestined before the foundation of the world, so if we know that we have been predestined for such a position, we have always to live according to the principles found in the Bible, the Word of God. We need to have other born-again Christians who can act as our 'sounding boards' and advisors to enlarge upon us what is on the mind and heart of God – like the prophets did in the Bible.

The positions I am focusing on are spiritual qualities which we (you and I) aspire to get as we hear God's Word and live by it. We are reaching upwards, heavenwards, to become an encouragement and support for people around us through our words and deeds, regardless of our titles.

Our Lord Jesus Christ is seated on the right hand of God, far above every title given to men and women and He is supporting every born-again Christian in His timeless, eternal prayers, so that His will and plans for mankind may be fulfilled and not hindered by powers and authorities of people who have titles but who are using them to oppress people under their authority.

**Jesus Christ is seated at the right hand of God, far above every title that can be given, not only in the present world but also in the one to come.**

As we know, there are titles that are familiar to all of us, but in the years or in the age to come, there will be titles that we presently know nothing about. The titles that will be given to people in the age to come will have powers and authorities but will always be below where Jesus Christ is seated; these powers and authorities will never be able to stop Jesus

Christ from accomplishing God's will and plans for humanity. Remember that our Lord Jesus Christ has been given the title or name that is above all titles, names in this present age, and in the one to come. And He has been given powers and authorities that are far above all powers and authorities in this age and in the one to come.

Turn now to Philippians2:9-10 as we teach more about the highest title, name, power and authority that Jesus Christ has been given. "Therefore God exalted Him to the highest place and gave Him the name that is above every name, that at the name of Jesus every knee should bow, in heaven and on earth, and every tongue confess that Jesus Christ is Lord to the glory of God the Father." Our Lord Jesus Christ, our Intercessor is the only One Who has been exalted in this world and in the world to come. And He is the only One Who has been given the title, the name that is above every name in this world and in the one to come. Although titled people throughout the earth may exalt themselves, Jesus Christ will always be on and have the highest position. The nature of mankind is so often self-seeking, being driven by a desire to be elevated and in some instances to be worshipped. But God is Almighty. He has purposed everything in heaven (angels), on earth (human beings), and under the earth(demons) to bow their knees at the name of Jesus Christ. And every tongue should confess that Jesus Christ is Lord to the glory of God the Father.

Even if antichrists and Satanists deny the Lordship of Jesus Christ, and even if they deny His highest position, designating it to someone else, the truth will remain the same. Truth is truth and Jesus Christ is able to defend Himself and make Himself known as the Only Lord and the Only One Who has the highest title or name that is above every name, or title, or power, or authority, or leader, or anything else in this present world and in the world to come. Ephesians 1:22 clearly reminds us that God placed all things (any name, any title, any power, any dominion, any authority, anything) under the feet of Jesus Christ; in other words we can say that God placed all things under the control of Jesus Christ and nothing can exalt itself above Him. And He cannot allow it to happen. Any name, or any title, or any power, or any dominion, or any authority, or any leader, or anything else will always be under the feet of Jesus: under the control of Jesus Christ in this world and the world to come. And all things being under His feet, under the control of Jesus Christ, will always enable Him to work without hindrance as He fulfils God's plan as it was ordained before the foundation of the world.

**Jesus Christ is Appointed to Be Head Over Everything of the Church – Ephesians1:22 Chapter 17**

Ephesians 1:22 says: “And God placed all things under His feet and appointed Him to be head of everything for the Church.”

*The Church Defined and Priorities* are taken from the material of Calvary Community Church on their course titled *‘Discipleship’*.

A. THE MEANING OF THE TERM

The word *church* is the translation of the Greek word *ekklesia* (ekklhsia). This word is composed of two parts. The first part (*ek*) means "*out of,*" and the last part (*klesia*) means "*called*". A church is a *called out* group of people; *an assembly*. The context will indicate the nature, purpose and function of the assembly being referred to.

B. THE NEW TESTAMENT CONCEPT

As the New Testament was being completed, there was a progression of revelation concerning the Church. One Bible scholar claims that at least 80 different images can be found in the New Testament to describe the Church. The Church is viewed as a family, a bride, a vineyard, a temple, a building, a flock, etc. But the most important designation of the Church in the New Testament is *"the Body of Christ"*. This metaphor communicates in a very dynamic way that the on-going activity of the Risen Christ is in and through the Church.

1. The beginning of the Church

The New Testament Church began its existence on the day of Pentecost. The description of the birth of the Church is found in Acts 2:1 -4. The Church, the Body of Christ, is entered by means of the baptism of the Holy Spirit (Colossians 1:24; I Corinthians 12:13). It is only logical to conclude that the Church could not be in existence before the baptizing ministry of the Holy Spirit was available. According to Acts 1:5, the Holy Spirit's baptism was still future after the resurrection of Christ. The only logical place to conclude that the Church was formed and the baptism of the Holy Spirit was initiated is Acts 2:1 -4. This is the event Peter looked back to as the fulfillment of Christ's promise of Spirit baptism (Acts 11:16).

2. The nature of the Church

Although the Church was a mystery before it was born (Ephesians 3:1 -11), its nature is revealed in the New Testament. In 1 Corinthians 12 the Church is described as a body. There are a number of characteristics which are immediately manifested in any well functioning body. The first one emphasized in I Corinthians 12 is that of unity. A healthy human body is a marvelous picture of coordination; every member in the body has its specific task to do. If a particular member does not do its work, the whole body suffers because of it.

The first eleven verses of this chapter demonstrate that the Holy Spirit has given a spiritual gift to every believer. The latter verses of this chapter emphasize that all these different gifts are to function in their rightful places; in other words, there is diversity in unity (verse 12). If the body is to do its job, all the necessary parts must be present and working.

We may not like the place that has been given to us in the body but we must carefully recognize that God is the One Who has given us our responsibility (verse 18). It also helps

to remember that even the most humble member is necessary for the well-being of the others (verse 22).
3. The future of the Church
The Church will be raptured when it is completed (1 Thessalonians 4:13ff; 1 Corinthians 15:51; 1 Thessalonians 1:10). In the future Messianic Kingdom, the Church will judge (1 Corinthians 6:2) and reign with Christ (2 Timothy 2:12; Revelation1:6 & 5:10).
So the Church, which is His body, is the group of believers baptized by the Holy Spirit into Christ and thus into His body, from the day of Pentecost until the rapture (Romans 12:5; 1 Corinthians 12:13; Ephesians 1:4-5; Galatians 3:27-28).
Note: Since the Church did not exist until the Day of Pentecost it cannot be found in the Old Testament. The phrase "Old Testament Church" is not a biblical one. The Church is entirely separate from the nation of Israel; the two are not to be identified in any way (see 1 Corinthians10:32; Philippians 3:20; Romans 11 ). The Church was not in existence during the earthly ministry of the Lord Jesus Christ. Our Lord states this when He predicted the formation of the Church in Matthew 16:18. The use of the future tense here confirms the truth of this statement.

**The Priorities of the Church**

In John 15 Jesus instructed His followers to carry out three priorities:
1. Verses 1 -11 -- "Abide in Me"
2. Verses 12-15 -- "Love one another"
3. Verses 16-27 -- "Bear witness of Me"

PRIORITY ONE: Upward -- The Lordship Of Christ
Scripture screams out the message that Christ is above all:
1. Colossians 1:15-17a All creation is His work and exists for Him:
2. Colossians 1:17b He holds it all together:
3. Colossians 1:18 He is Head and Source of the Church.

But how do we practice the Lordship of Christ?
1. Obedience -- follow His instructions (John 14:23; 16:13)
2. Worship



According to I Peter 2:4-9, as members of His Church we are priests who are to be offering up spiritual sacrifices to God. What spiritual sacrifices are we to be offering up?
• Hebrews 13:15: "Through Jesus, therefore, let us continually offer to God a sacrifice of praise- the fruit of lips that confess His name."
• Hebrews 13:16: "And do not forget to do good and to share with others, for with such sacrifices God is well pleased."
• Romans 15:16: "To be a minister of God to the Gentiles with the priestly duty of proclaiming the Gospel of God, so that the Gentiles might become an offering acceptable to God, sanctified by the Holy Spirit."
• Philippians 2:17: "But even if I am being poured out like a drink offering on the sacrifice and service coming from your faith, I am glad and rejoice with all of you."
• Romans 12:1 -2: "Therefore, I urge you, brothers, in view of God's mercy, to offer your bodies as living sacrifices, holy and pleasing to God- this is your spiritual act of worship. Do not conform any longer to the pattern of this world, but be transformed

by the renewing of your mind. Then you will be able to test and approve what God's will is- His good, pleasant and perfect will."

PRIORITY TWO: Inward -- Love One Another

This flows out of priority number one (2 Corinthians 8:5). This is the fulfillment of the New Commandment which Jesus left us (John 13:34).

PRIORITY THREE: Outward -- Bear Witness to the World

• This priority flows out of the first two (John 13:34-35).

We have finished learning about the definition and priorities of the Church from the material given to me by Rev James Robinette and written by Calvary Community Church.

Let us look again to our main verse in Ephesians 1:22 "And God placed all things under His feet and appointed Him to be head of everything for the Church."

Let us continue to develop Chapter 17 of this book, looking into the following revealed matters concerning the Church.

**God appointed Jesus Christ to be head of everything for the Church.**

Jesus Christ is the Head of the Church, the Body of Christ. He is the Head of every human being who has received Him as Lord and Saviour. He knows in full what God purposed for the Church, you and I, if we have received Him as Lord and Saviour. He has many ways that He uses as He has the direction of the Church. Nothing, no-one or no power can hinder Him from accomplishing God's purpose for the Church. Any local church can start with two or three members but if it is in God's plan it will grow and expand around the nations of the world, even though it can start without any visible source of people or financial support for its success.

Let us think about the first Church that was born on the Day of Pentecost as it spread during the persecution of the apostles and disciples of Jesus Christ.

"The apostles performed many miraculous signs and wonders among the people. And all the believers used to meet together in Solomon's Colonnade. No-one else dared join them, even though they were highly regarded by people. Nevertheless, more and more men and women believed in the Lord and were added to their number. As a result, people brought the sick into the streets and laid them on beds and mats so that at least Peter's shadow might fall on some of them as he passed by. Crowds gathered also from the towns around Jerusalem, bringing their sick and those tormented by evil spirits, and all of them were healed. Then the high priest and his associates, who were members of the party of the Sadducees, were filled with jealousy. They arrested the apostles and put them in the public jail. But during the night an angel of the Lord opened the doors of the jail and brought them out. 'Go, stand in the temple courts', He said, 'and tell the people the full message of the new life'" (Acts5:12-20).

The Church of Jesus Christ started as a group numbering about one hundred and twenty, as recorded in Acts 1:15. Verse 14 of this same book says that the members of this group joined together constantly in prayer, along with the women and Mary, the mother of Jesus Christ, and with His brothers. Then in Acts 2:14-41 we discover that the apostle Peter preached his first message to the people, and as a result about three thousand accepted his message and were added to their number that day.

A small group became in one day a large group, numbering about three thousand, plus the first small group of a hundred and twenty disciples of Jesus Christ. This group of believers is the Church that I am speaking about in this book. And Jesus Christ is the Head, Director of this group of believers, the Church, the Body of Christ.
Acts 4:12 begins with this sentence: "The apostles performed many miraculous signs and wonders among the people."
The number of those who were added to the group of believers is not mentioned in Acts 5:12-20 but there were a large number of people from all directions that were being added every day to the group of believers, the Church. Jesus Christ used a method of performing many miraculous signs and wonders among people as He was looking for new members who could be added to His group, the Church. Praise God, there is no method that Jesus Christ can choose to use and fail to accomplish His purpose for His Church? Any method He uses leads Him to success and victory.
As we continue with Acts5:14 we will discover that more and more men and women believed in the Lord and were added to their number. This group of believers, the Church, became a daily conquering mighty army of the Lord Jesus Christ as He was using His vessel, the group of believers in Christ, the Church. They became a highly regarded group by people, and even today any group of believers who put Jesus Christ first in their lives as the Head, the Director of believers, they too are highly regarded as God uses them mightily. Titled people such as pastors and priests have to know that they are not the Head of the Church but that Jesus Christ is the ***only*** Head and they are only servants of God under the leadership of Jesus Christ. Pastors and priests are positioned as ambassadors; they represent Him as they execute His commands in His Word. Jesus Christ is the ***only*** One Who knows the needs of every member of His group of believers, the Church, His Body. And He is the ***only*** One Who knows which means can be used as He responds to every need in His Church. The church we (you and I) are pastoring is not our church but it is the Church headed by Jesus Christ, and we pastors are His servants who fulfil His will and plans for His Church. As pastors serve the group of believers of Jesus Christ, the Church, the result of the growth will always be amazing, just as it was in Acts 5:15-16: "As a result, people brought the sick into the streets and laid them on beds and mats so that at least Peter's shadow might fall on some of them as he passed by. Crowds gathered also from the towns around Jerusalem, bringing their sick and those tormented by evil spirits, and all of them were healed."
Jesus Christ uses mightily those who recognize Him as Head of everything for the Church. The peoples of the world, though mostly ignorant to the truth, are in need of such groups of believers because they have given up hope and see no purpose for life. The world desperately needs healing. It needs to be able to "bring the sick into the streets and lay them on beds and mats so that at least our shadow might fall on some of them, bringing healing as we pass by", just as it did for Peter. People who have lost hope around the nations of the world need to hear about such a group of believers of Jesus Christ so He can solve their needs and problems through His servants. People need to be exposed to a group

of believers of Jesus Christ in which they can be healed, strengthened and ignited spiritually as they hear Christ's message, the Word of God. Jesus said He came to give us life more abundantly (John 10:10) and that abundant life is for all who will call upon His name – the hopeless, the weak, the broken-hearted –Jesus Christ is the answer to every need.

Those who have lost hope need to be encouraged to join a group in which they will receive hope. And people without spiritual support need to have support from believers so they can hear the message of Jesus Christ, Who is a support to anyone who has no support. As the transforming message about Jesus Christ is being preached and taught in a group of believers, many other people will come to join that group, the Church, so that they too can be transformed through the powerful Word of God preached and taught in the Christian meeting - Acts 5:16: "Crowds gathered also from the towns around Jerusalem, bringing their sick and those tormented by evil spirits, and all of them were healed."

While we continue to develop our topic of Jesus Christ being appointed by God to be the Head of everything for the Church, allow me to use myself as an example, as we consider God's vision for our individual lives. When God plants a global vision in someone's heart, a seed through which He will impact thousands of people around the nations of the world, it starts with just a thought, an idea that comes into your mind. But when that man or woman takes action, as I am doing daily, week by week, month by month, and year by year, the vision will grow to impact thousands of people who join churches and ministries. God uses those small groups of believers that He first chose to multiply His Church, for His glory. A church may be birthed with just two or three people but if Jesus Christ is Head of that group the positive impact will be the sign of Jesus Christ being the Head of everything for it, even though the impact of this small group may take time to develop.

Let us conclude this chapter as we look at the persecution and opposition to the group - the believers of Jesus Christ.

Acts 5:17-20: "Then the high priest and his associates, who were members of the party of the Sadducees, were filled with jealousy. They arrested the apostles and put them in the public jail. But during the night an angel of the Lord opened the doors of the jail and brought them out. 'Go, stand in the temple courts', he said, 'and tell the people the full message of the new life.'"

This religious group called the Sadducees were filled with envy as they saw the results of the work of the apostles. The Sadducees opposed the apostles, fiercely persecuting them in the hope of stamping out this 'new religion'. But Jesus Christ, Who is the Head of the Church, sent His angel during the night to open the locked doors of the public jail in which the apostles were imprisoned, bringing them out through miraculous provision. This confirms that God is always sending His angels to open closed doors for us: doors of obstacles in our lives, churches and other businesses, but doors that have been predestined by God to be opened. We see that the apostles, the pillars of the Church, were at that time persecuted for the purpose of destroying the Church. But God opened the closed doors of the prison: the closed doors for proclaiming the message of Jesus Christ, the Head of the Church. And even these days He still opens closed doors for the operation of His Church in any area in which His group, the Church, is faithfully serving Him. God opens new doors that no-one, no power nor any authority can close, just as the angel of our Lord Jesus Christ opened the prison doors, telling them to "Go and stand in the temple courts, and tell the people the full message of the new life found in Jesus Christ."

If people read the history of the Church in every generation they will discover that persecution and opposition have always been present but that Jesus Christ has always been the Head of the Church. And, remember that God purifies His people, the Church, through suffering so He can make us stronger in the faith, like pure gold that has been purified through fire. Wars and other disasters may destroy churches, temples or houses in which believers of Jesus Christ meet to worship and praise Him; circumstances and hardships may scatter the believers of Jesus Christ, but the Lord is still their Head and He is still pursuing His purposes for every member of His body, regardless of the circumstances they are passing through. It is evident from scripture that hardships, no matter in what form they come, will bring us closer to Jesus if we maintain our faith at every step along life's journey.

Let us learn through the story of Joseph in the book of Genesis 37:5:"One night Joseph had a dream, and when he told his brothers about it, they hated him more than ever."

And verse9 of this same chapter says that: "Soon Joseph had another dream, and again he told his brothers about it. 'Listen, I have had another dream,' he said: 'The sun, the moon, and eleven stars bowed low before me.'"

Joseph had a dream of becoming a king, and his father, his mother, and his eleven brothers bowed low before him as he became their superior, their support. Joseph was his father's favourite son, so when his brothers heard his dreams they despised and hated him more than ever: such was their hatred toward him that they plotted to kill him. But God made a way and, instead of slaying him, they sold him as a slave to the Ishmaelites, who in turn sold him in Egypt to Pharaoh's captain of the guard, Potiphar.

And so it was that Potiphar's wife lustfully desired Joseph, but when her deceitful plan failed she took revenge and became a false witness against him. He, though innocent, was then cast into prison. But God! The God he feared and loved was with him as he passed through many kinds of hardships. He was a stranger in a foreign land, where they spoke a foreign language, where his cries of innocence went unheard, but he faithfully continued to trust in God, even in the confinement of a prison.

Then came the day when the prophetic dreams of his youth came to pass. Through God's divine gift of the *interpreting of dreams,* Joseph was elevated to become the Prime Minister of Egypt when he interpreted Pharaoh's God-given dreams - the coming drought and famine in the country and its surrounding neighbours, including Israel. Not only did Joseph interpret the dreams but he also gave them God's divine plan to store up much food in the seven years of plenty. And so it was that Joseph's brothers came to Egypt seeking food at the command of their father, Jacob, and unknowingly bowed low before their brother for life's sustenance. This beautiful Bible illustration that started off as a torrent of hate, became a wonderful love story because of one person who dared to allow the hardships of life mould him into a victorious winner. What a reunion it must have been when he came face-to-face

with his father and full blood-brother Benjamin!
I remember now the hardships that I passed through when I was at Kampala for my theological training. Despite experiencing many obstacles and trials, I completed my studies because I trusted God and God made the way for my success, just as He is doing now as I am pursuing to fulfil His vision for my life - that of planting churches around the nations of the world as we minister to hopeless people, beginning in Beni in the Democratic Republic of Congo. And the fear of God within our hearts is enabling us as we trust Him to supply our daily needs.
I have shared with you the story of Joseph so that I may illustrate the topic of this chapter *Jesus Christ being appointed by God to be the Head of everything for the Church* - and He uses and chooses whatever means, so that He can fulfil God's plans for every member of the Church, regardless of the circumstances. May we always be mindful that Jesus Christ is working day and night on God's plans and purposes for your life and my life, so that we will be like Him, regardless of the circumstances we are passing through. He is preparing His Church like a bride, and He will soon come and live forever with His church, the believers of Jesus Christ. And all the glory will continue to be to Him because nothing will hinder Him from accomplishing God's will or plan for you and I, the Church.

**Jesus Christ Fills and Completes Everything for the Church By Himself – Ephesians1:23 Chapter 18**

We begin this last chapter of the book by reading Ephesians 1:23: ". . . which is His body, the fullness of Him Who fills everything in every way."

We have learned in the previous chapter that God appointed Jesus Christ to be the Head of the Church. And in this last chapter we will learn how Jesus Christ fills and makes everything for the Church by Himself.

In this chapter I will develop two points:

• Jesus Christ fills everything for the Church by Himself.

• Jesus Christ makes complete everything for the Church by Himself.

**Jesus Christ fills everything for the Church by Himself.**

The words *"everything for the Church"* can also be interpreted as *"the parts of the Church."* This verse says that the Church is the Body of Jesus Christ, and this body has parts called "all believers of Jesus Christ." God's purpose for every part of Jesus' body is to make it full by Jesus Christ Himself. Are we aware that before we receive Jesus Christ we are filled by thoughts that we inherit from people and from Satan? Everyone who is not born-again is filled by evil thoughts inherited from evil people. And these evil thoughts always influence people to act as evil people because they are filled by evil thoughts they inherit from Satan and evil people around them. These evil thoughts push people to fulfil Satan's evil will and plan, which do not bring glory to God.

As soon as we (you and I) receive Jesus Christ as Lord and Saviour, Jesus Christ begins to fulfil God's plan for our lives of filling us by Jesus Himself, so that our minds can be filled with divine thoughts, the Word of God. And as we become daily filled by Jesus Christ we begin to think according to God's will, and we bring glory to Him through our thoughts and actions.

John 1:1-4 clearly teaches us that Jesus Christ is the Word: "In the beginning was the Word, and the Word was with God, and the Word was God. He was with God in the beginning. Through Him all things were made; without Him nothing was made that has been made. In Him was life, and that life was the light of men."

This Word is Jesus Christ and it is a Living Word. Once Jesus Christ fills every part of His body by Himself, every part of His body becomes a living part like Jesus Christ Himself. And this living part (you and I) brings life to people who are around us. Our words and actions have to bring life to people around us because we (you and I) are filled by Himself, Who is real life. Jesus Christ is life and He fills us with life, which will then overflow to other people who have no life within them.

We have to be flexible to Jesus Christ so that He can fill us by Himself. To be flexible to Jesus means that we have to always hear His Word and do what He tells us to do. As we hear Him speak through His Word, and do whatever He tells us to do, regardless of the circumstances, Jesus Christ is filling us by Himself, knowing or without knowing about it. ,And, as a result, the fullness of Jesus Christ within us begins to overflow through us to other people as we become the real ambassadors of Jesus Christ here on earth.

Jesus Christ, Who is the Word of God, filled His apostles by Himself as they were learning from Him daily for three years. And as the result of their being filled by Jesus Christ Himself, they gave spiritual life to those who had no life, including you and I, because we received the Good News from people who were taught by other people, who received the Good News from the apostles from generation to generation. And from generation to generation people are receiving the Word of God from those who have been filled by Jesus Christ Himself: thus we are preaching and teaching people daily so that they might be filled by Jesus Christ, the Word of God.

Let us now start the second point of this chapter.

**• Jesus Christ makes complete everything for the Church by Himself.**

God's plans and purposes for every born-again Christian are to make complete every part of the Body of Christ by Jesus Himself. To be complete means to be mature. Any born-again Christian should grow spiritually as Jesus Christ, the Word of God, fills him or her by Himself, to the point that we reach the same understanding of Jesus that His apostles had of Him. They understood Who Jesus is, what He came for, the mission He gave them, and how they could accomplish it, regardless of the circumstances. The victories experienced by the apostles and disciples of Jesus are recorded in scripture for the purpose and encouragement of spurring on the faith of Christians everywhere.

Jesus Christ is God Himself, Who loves lost sinners, and Who gave Himself for all mankind when He died on the cross like a criminal as our substitute. This Agape (Christ-like) love was poured into the hearts of the apostles and the disciples of Jesus Christ, and this love provoked them to being committed to preach the Good News of Jesus Christ, regardless of the circumstances. Many of the followers of Jesus Christ did not consider their own lives to be of greater importance than that of fulfilling the tasks given to them by the Lord Himself.

The apostle Paul was a man chosen by God as an instrument to carry Jesus' name before the Gentiles and their kings, and before the people of Israel. And Jesus Christ said of Paul: "I will show him how he must suffer for My name" (Acts9:15-16). From the moment Paul (then Saul of Tarsus) was stopped from his murderous intentions on the road to Damascus, Jesus Christ began to reveal Himself to him, filling Paul with Himself through the Word of God, through the power of the Holy Spirit, through a vision and through the restoration of his eyesight, which the Lord had withheld from him for three days while he was being made complete, fully immersed in the presence of Jesus.

His being complete enabled him to be used by God as a chosen instrument to carry the name of Jesus Christ before the Gentiles and their kings, and before the people of Israel. It was not an easy journey, as Jesus had prophesied of him, "He will suffer many things for My name's sake." But, no matter how difficult and perilous the circumstances, from shipwrecks to imprisonment, he endured, accomplishing God's mission for his life because he was already made complete by Jesus Christ Himself (see 2 Corinthians 11:23-33).

Paul was an exhorter, authoring books and letters to strengthen and encourage the churches, despite the fact that he was passing through more sufferings than those to whom he sent his writings, which were filled with words of exhortation and comfort. He was fully mature in God, knowing that the hardships we pass through are not to be compared to the glory we will have in the coming world. Jesus Christ told His disciples that: "You will have troubles (problems and trials) but do not give up for I have won (overcome) the world."

Born-again Christians who are filled and complete by Jesus Christ Himself cannot give up when we meet with suffering (problems and trials). We have to know and believe that Jesus Christ is beside us and nothing will hinder us from accomplishing the task God has given us to do. And we should be assured that the glory we shall have in the coming kingdom is far greater and not to be compared to our present suffering.

Dear brothers and sisters in the Lord Jesus Christ, may you allow me to conclude this chapter by saying that suffering is part of God's plan for our life and we have to consider that our present sufferings are not worth comparing with the glory that will be revealed in us as we continue to endure: as we commit ourselves to living God's will and plans for our life, regardless of circumstances. We must not give up when we meet with problems and trials because, if God has allowed them to happen in life, it is because He wants to use them as means that will lead us to our being filled and complete in Jesus Christ. These seemingly negative events in our life are doorways into God's miraculous provision that He uses to make us stronger and stronger in Him because we know that: "In ***all things*** God works for the good of those who love Him, who have been called according to His purpose" (Romans 8:28).

So we should rejoice in our sufferings, as the apostle Paul says in Romans 5:3-5: "Not only so, but we also rejoice in our sufferings, because we know that suffering produces perseverance; perseverance, character; and character hope. And hope does not disappoint us, because God has poured out His love into our hearts by His Holy Spirit, Whom He has given us."

## Conclusion

I conclude this book by firstly sharing a few personal words regarding the plan and purposes of God for my life. I am now a Visionary and Senior Pastor of Ebenezer Evangelical Church International. We have a vision of planting churches around the nations of the world, ministering to people who have lost hope, and the fear of God is enabling us to do it as we trust Him to supply all our daily needs according to His riches in Christ Jesus. Since I first responded to the universal invitation of receiving Jesus Christ as Lord and Saviour, I have learned to do always what he tells me to do in a committed way and at the proper time: thus He always reveals to me His will for my life as He provides for my daily needs and the needs of our church. As I have continued to live by faith, serving Him, I have discovered that I am not only a Senior Pastor but I am also a writer of books and articles. I believe that as I continue to serve Him faithfully, He will once again reveal to me His unfolding, additional plan for my life.

In the same way, all who have received Jesus Christ as Lord and Saviour, and are doing what God is telling them to do in a committed way without excuses and in the proper time set by God, He will always reveal to them His additional plans for their lives.

People who have received Jesus Christ as Lord and Saviour are called *saints*, children of God. However we can suffer also for the Lord's sake but our suffering does not have to cause us to live like children of the darkness. Even in the time of our suffering we should maintain our holiness as we look to the Author and Finisher of our faith, Jesus Christ, Who suffered intensely, but did not sin (Hebrews 12:2).

God is calling every follower of Jesus Christ to be faithful to Him, regardless of the increase of wickedness and opposing circumstances all around us. As we continue to stand firm in our daily walk, our God will save us; He will welcome us to enter into His banquet; we will rejoice with Him, and He will say to us: "Good and faithful servant."

Be encouraged to search the Scriptures always, being committed to do whatever God tells you to do, and in the proper time set by God, then He will always reveal to you His additional plan for your life. He will open up opportunities that lead you to every blessing He has for you in Christ Jesus as He rewards you for being obedient to Him. Our blessings are in Christ Jesus, so Jesus Christ has to be our Master so that these blessings can be available to us.

Dear ones in the Lord Jesus, do your part in accomplishing God's plans for your life and God will always be faithful to do His part. The peoples of the world are becoming hopeless and in despair because of the sufferings and hardships they are passing through. But their becoming hopeless will not alarm God and cause Him to fail to accomplish the good plans He has for them: plans that will give them a future and a hope, regardless of what they are passing through.

You are a predestined son or daughter of God, so if you have not already, may you receive

Jesus Christ as Lord and Saviour and become a child of God. This will enable God to fulfil His plans for your life as you become united with Him as soon as you receive Jesus Christ as Lord and Saviour.

The book of John 1:12-13 says:"Yet to all who received Him, Jesus Christ, to those who believed in His name, He gave the right to become children of God-children born not of natural descent, nor human decision or a husband's will, but born of God."

You are now a child of God by God's decision and in accordance with His pleasure and His will, and once God adopts you as His own, He will no longer disown you. He made us His sons and daughters with all wisdom and understanding. But He expects us to be sons and daughters who will always do whatever He tells us to do in a committed way and in the proper time set by God because "There is time and season for every activity under the sun" (Ecclesiastes 3:1). When we do what God tells us to do in a committed way and in the proper time, praising Him through our actions and speech, we bring glory and honour to His name.

Let us continue to search for the Lord and be committed to what He is telling us, because what He is instructing us to do are mysterious means through which God fulfils His plans and purposes for our lives. And as we use these mysterious means through which God fulfils His plans and purposes, many people around us will come to Jesus Christ when they see the marvellous things God is doing through us, the ambassadors of Jesus Christ here on earth.

The truth is that it is God's pleasure to reveal to you and me His mysterious plans regarding Christ and the wonderful intertwining of Himself in our life.

Because we are predestined according to the plan of God, Who works out everything for the fulfilment of His plan through Jesus Christ, so we should always receive faith from its source: "So then faith comes by hearing, that is by hearing the Word of God" (Romans 10:17). We should always live by faith because God is pleased by faith and He rewards those who earnestly seek Him by faith. However God is not pleased by people who live by sight, only believing what they can visually see; He cannot reward them as they seek Him without faith.

The reward that God gives to those who sincerely seek Him by faith is beyond the understanding of people who do not *walk the walk of faith*. The means God uses as He rewards those who are living by faith as they hear God's Word and do whatever they hear from Him, are special means that always lead to victory and success.

Dear brothers and sisters, we are purposed for the praise of the glory of Jesus Christ. We are what we are by God's grace, and we have what we possess by the ability Jesus is giving us because the Bible says that 'God is the One Who gives you the ability and the strength to make your riches.' Let us continue to praise Jesus for what we are and for the riches we have then the glory will always be to God. And, once He becomes glorified through us in whatever we proclaim, He will continue to increase our wisdom and He will continue to bless us wherever we live, and He will bless whatever we do. Because He desires to be praised in every provision, be they large or small, He will always bless us when we exalt His sacred name for that which we are and that which we possess.

Let us serve Jesus Christ without excuses. Let us live the rest of our life here on earth for Christ and not for ourselves. He has adopted us into His family, and there is a reward, an inheritance for those who are included in Christ Jesus.

The heart of God is for all peoples to respond to His glorious Gospel of Salvation, be it via TV, radio, literature, preaching, teaching, one-on-one witnessing, etc., for God will never disappoint those who come to Him and His Good News. He has prepared an inheritance for those who will call upon His name and be saved. He never gives up on His plan. It is the reason why He cannot stop connecting with you. It is the reason why men and women of God will support you in their daily prayers so that God can fulfil His wonderful plans concerning you. And God will enable you too to be a prayerful man or woman if you are willing.

Most great men and women of God are prayerful people and they have other prayerful men and women of God who are supporting them in prayer. Even other people who are great around the nations of the world and who do not know God can become also great because of the prayer support of the members of their families: the grace of God can reach any human being.

Men and women of God from around the globe are remembering our nations in their daily prayers, praying for peace to return in South Sudan, Burundi, Democratic Republic of Congo and other war-torn nations, and as a result we are experiencing the daily impact of their prayers. I believe we will soon see far-reaching amazing results from their prayers because God has plans for nations and the peoples within these nations that are bogged down in wars and other hardships.

The power of prayer is often invisible to our natural eyes but its results are usually clearly seen. Those who live by faith are also prayerful people and the results of their faith bring wonderful outcomes and answers to their prayers. If men and women of God share about the power of answered prayer, how the invisible things become visible, we cannot help but give the glory to God. Are we available to support others in prayer?

We need also wisdom and revelation from God so that we can know God better. And as we know Him better we will experience an increase in wisdom and revelation from Him. When we search for God with all our heart, when we pray and meditate upon His Word, we will be filled with His glorious presence. Have you ever wondered why many people neglect God's business of preaching the Gospel? Could it be because they don't have wisdom and revelation which can lead them to know God better? Could it be they have misunderstood God because of their lack of wisdom and revelation that could lead them to know God better?

In East Africa and in some other parts of the world many people are committed in serving God and financially supporting God's business of preaching and teaching the Gospel. But here in the Democratic Republic of Congo it is the opposite: only few are committed in serving the Lord, and only few support God's business with much money: only few parents encourage their children to go for theological training and become fulltime ministers of God and His life-giving Gospel.

It is my belief that the reason why parents do not encourage their children to go for theological training is because these parents are lacking wisdom and revelation that can lead them to a better knowledge of God. An increase of God's wisdom and revelation will always propel us to give the Lord's work the highest and first priority in our life – our commitment, our time, our giving.

My prayer is that God may enlighten the eyes of your heart; that you may know the hope to which He has called you. May He enlighten the eyes of your heart so you may recognize the riches of God's glorious inheritance within you. People love God more because of the knowledge of Him and the knowledge they have for themselves, as they see God and themselves with the eyes of their heart.

God's incomparably great wonder-working power can do what we cannot do and what we cannot imagine. It can do what is beyond our understanding. It can cause to happen whatever God wants to perform without anyone, anything, and any force hindering Him from accomplishing what He has in mind. God's wonder-working power is able to change and transform any circumstance around us as He pursues to fulfil His purposes for our life, our family, our Christian organization, our business, our nation and our world. This incomparably great wonder- working power is able to move mountains, making impossible situations possible: rendering obstacles powerless to annihilate the Lord God's will.

This power is able to make rivers in the desert as God makes a way where it seems there is no way: as He opens opportunities for yours and my successes and victories. It is able to make a poor man rich. It is able to change a beggar into someone who can be a support to thousands of people. It is able to heal every sickness and able to heal any broken heart.

This incomparably great power for us who believe is able to accomplish God's will for us in His time, regardless of the circumstances. Let us continue to pray so that this incomparably great power can be known by us, and let us always be available to God so that this incomparably great wonder-working power can always accomplish God's perfect plans within us and through us.

May we always be mindful that our Lord Jesus Christ has been given the title or name that is above all titles, above all names in this present world and in the one to come; He has been given powers and authorities that are far above all powers and authorities in this world and in the one to come. Philippians 2:9-10 emphasizes the fact that "God exalted Him to the highest place and gave Him the name that is above every name, that at the name of Jesus every knee should bow, in heaven and on earth, and every tongue confess that Jesus Christ is Lord to the glory of God the Father."

Our Lord Jesus Christ, our Intercessor, is the ***only*** One who has been exalted in this present world and in the one to come. He is the ***only*** One Who has been given the title, name that is above every name in this present world and in the one to come. His title, King of kings and Lord of lords, overrides any man-made title in this world: He alone qualifies to be given the highest position because He was and is exalted by God the Father, Who changes not.

Although people and the devil himself may crave worship through human beings, Almighty God has purposed everything in heaven (angels), on earth (human beings), and under the earth(demons) to bow their knees at the name of Jesus Christ. And that every tongue should confess that Jesus Christ is Lord, to the glory of God the Father. Even if antichrists and Satanists deny the Lordship of Jesus Christ, and even if they deny His highest position and delegate it to someone else, the truth will remain the same because Jesus Christ is able to defend Himself and make Himself known as the ***only*** Lord and the ***only*** One Who has the highest title or name that is above every name, or title, or power, or authority, or leader, or anything else in this present world and in the world to come. God has placed all things – names, titles, powers, dominions, authorities, everything – under the feet of Jesus Christ (Ephesians 1:22). In other words we can say that God placed all things under the control of Jesus Christ and nothing can exalt itself above Him. He cannot allow it to happen. Any name, or any title, or any power, or any dominion, or any authority, or any leader, or anything else will always be under the feet of Jesus Christ in this present world and in the world to come. And all things, being under the feet of Jesus Christ, will always enable Him to work without hindrances, as He fulfils God's plan as it was ordained before the foundation of the world.

Yes, we can rejoice in the fact that Jesus Christ is working on God's plans and purposes day and night so that we will be like Him, regardless of the circumstances we may be passing through. He is preparing His Church like a bride, and He will soon come and live forever with His Church, the believers of Jesus Christ. And all the glory will continue to be to Him because nothing will hinder Him from accomplishing God's will or plan for you and I, the Church.

Dear brothers and sisters in the Lord Jesus Christ, allow me to conclude this book by again saying that suffering is part of God's plan for our life and we have to consider that our present sufferings are not worth comparing with the glory that will be revealed in us, you and I, as we continue to endure these difficult times. We must commit ourselves in accomplishing God's plans for our life, the vision or mission God has given us. We must put on the whole armour of God (Ephesians 6:7-10) so we will not give up when we are faced with trials and problems, for we know that "In all things God works for the good of those who love Him, who have been called according to His purpose" (Romans 8:28). We should rejoice in our suffering because "we know that suffering produces perseverance; perseverance, character; and character hope. And hope does not disappoint us, because God has poured out His love into our hearts by His Holy Spirit, Whom He has given us" (Romans 5:3-5).

**May you pray this prayer as you ask God to fulfil His plan for your life.**

**"Father God, here I am to ask You to bless me abundantly. May You fulfil Your plan for my**

**life as You open daily for me opportunities through Your Word. May You enable me to do**

**whatever You ask of me in a committed way and in the proper time set by You, my God, so that I can be successful and victorious all the days of my life. I give You permission to fulfil Your plan and purposes for my good that will give me a future and a hope. In Jesus' name. Amen."**

## THE TESTIMONY OF THE MAN OF GOD: MAHAMBA WA-IBERA EVARISTE & HIS WIFE ELIZABETH

He was born on 5th August 1984, and after his birth his parents rented a house in which there were demons although they did know about it. People who were living in that house were being attacked by those evil spirits. And as a result that building remained there as an abandoned dwelling place.

His father looked for a house in which they could live in and he got a house that belonged to a man who was practicing human sacrifice.

One day when Pastor Wa-ibera's mother was coming from the field, as she carried him (while he was still a baby), she found him in a convulsion. Then all the neighbours surrounded her as they were telling her that they were sorry for not telling her about the wrong house in which she lived.

Pastor Mahamba Wa-ibera's parents paid a lot of money for his medicine and, as a result he was healed miraculously. He lived from his birth until 2004 while he was separated from God and he did not mind about religious meetings.

He was born-again by the Holy Spirit on 27th June 2004 after hearing a message on the pillar of cloud that was leading the Israelites at day time, and at night leading them as a pillar of fire when they were coming from Egypt.

He became a committed singer after his conversion, and three months later he received a call from God for pastoring. And then he planted a church in 2004 as a response to God's call. And then he went for a theological training in Kampala, Uganda.

He received a vision from God in 2004 for planting churches around the world as he ministers to people who have no hope. This vision was launched on 8th February 2014 as he applied the wonderful insights within the writing "Fulfilling the Vision from God" of the man of God, Rodney W. Francis.

He is serving the Lord as the founder and senior pastor of Ebenezer Evangelical Church International. He is based in Beni, DR Congo and his wife Elizabeth is a great spiritual support to him.

God is using him mightily in healing the sick.

God has blessed him with his first child daughter Mahamba Kyota- Nyota Thanks and his first son Mahamba Kyota Moses.

The ministry that he is coordinating is an Equipping Training Church. And it is now impacting amazingly the smallest and largest denominations in DRC as their members are being equipped with the insights within the Word of God. He is also working as the DRC Regional Director of Head Stone Ministries and the DRC Representative of Gospel Faith Messenger Ministry. He is training also farmers as we works the country manager of Warm Heart DR Congo.

# WARM HEART DR CONGO

Warm Heart DR Congo is a Nonprofit Organization, a group of committed people working together to bring positive change and improve the lives the poor communities of the Democratic Republic of Congo as we are recognized Warm Heart Worldwide ; a Nonprofit Organazation based in the United States of America.

Warm Heart DR Congo is the local representative of Warm Heart Worldwide, INC. ( EIN 26-2059241), an American IRS recognized taxe exempt 501.C.3 nonprofit, registered in the USA. Warm Heart DR Congo « W.H.DRC » is recognized by Warm Heart Worldwide. Under the direction of Pastor Mahamba Wa-ibera Evariste Warm Heart DRC is a Nationalist Expression of the desire to improve the lives of poor Congolese citizens. We are engaged in the pursuit of the sustainable development goals. So Warm Heart DRC has no political, religious or other discruptive, discriminatory ends. Dr Michael Shafer and MS. Evelind A. Schecter are Co- Founders and Co- Directors of Warm Heart Worldwide, INC. Pastor Mahamba Wa-ibera Evariste has served as the Warm Heart DR Congo Country Manager since August 2021. Warm Heart DR Congo fights against climate change and for greater food security for the smallholders of the Democratic Republic of Congo. We teach poor farmers how to make and use biochar to cool the climate, clean the environment, improve the public health, reduce rural poverty and training how to build houses that are carbon sinks as we fight against the climate change and the global warming. We are training small farmers about biochar and how to prevent the Global Warming and Climate Change, and to improve the environment. Our main focus is on children that live in isolated villages, isolated by distance, language, and opportunities. Without our help they would remain isolated, uneducated, and follow the footsteps of their families to live a life of poverty. With our help, these children are learning the language of the World outside their village. They are getting an education. Once a child joins Warm Heart family there are no bounds to their opportunities in life. We see our kids through their full potential, including a college education. We have a staff dedicated people in DRC to help us reach our goals. Our DRC Board of Directors are caring people who have made a commitment to the success of our program. Volunteers are the backbone of Warm Heart DR Congo . People who care and want to make a difference by helping others.

**Warm Heart Funding Sources**

Warm Heart DR Congo receives no financial support from Warm Heart Worldwide for any aspect of its work. Strategic Partners help us with projects beyond our scope of operations. Warm Heart depends on funds and work donations from people who want to make a difference in the World, and recognize that even a small donation can have a huge impact on improving the lives of others.

**Vision of Warm Heart DR Congo**

We envision a world in which rural communities offer members sustainable lives hoods and generational well- being.

**Our Mission**

We are able to help marginalized and forgotten communities to become educated, connected and empowered to create a better World.

Printed by Books on Demand GmbH, Norderstedt / Germany